Camp of Death

The Donner Party Mountain Camp
1846 - 47

by J. Quinn Thornton

EDITOR'S PREFACE

Except for newspaper stories, the chapters in this book were the first published account of the Donner Party disaster of 1846 and 1847. They were published in 1849 in New York by Harper & Brothers, in a 2-volume book dealing mainly with other matters of interest to emigrants, settlers, and prospectors in or on their way to the subject area: "Oregon and California in 1848." This was soon enough to the time of the Donner Party's suffering that the 44 survivors were still recovering from both the physical and mental effects of their ordeal, in which 36 of their companions died, some to be eaten to sustain the still living.

Author Thornton's record has good consistency with those published later, although he is harder on the last survivor of the Mountain Camp, branding him for life as a cannibal by choice, perhaps too severe when one considers the harsh circumstances that might ameliorate such a judgement.

It has become trite in introducing the Donner Party story to contrast their plight with modern times when a transcontinental railroad and highway carry us in comfort past the once-isolated camp. But this forgets that the winters of the mid-1800s were snowier than today's—during that period glaciers were growing throughout the world and of course in the Sierra Nevada. Now they are shrinking, and the few times recently we have had severe winters, even our arterials have been blocked. No, the Donner Party faced a scene and situation even worse than may be imagined by reference to today's winters.

Thornton's story is grotesque, gory, and, tragic horror—a negative chapter in the Winning of the West made all the worse because it is true history and therefore important in understanding our roots.

William R. Jones
Series Editor

Note: Author Thornton became first supreme judge of Oregon.

THE CAMP OF DEATH.

This frontispiece illustration was also the frontispiece for the original 1849 edition of this account of the Donner Party. "The Camp of Death" caption used here is the same as the original caption, too. Author Thornton's "Camp of Death" was on the Sierra Nevada's western slope, where 4 emigrants died when snowbound while trying to reach safety after fleeing "The Mountain Camp" at Donner Lake. The title of this reprinting takes editorial license in applying "camp of death" to the experiences of the Donner Party as a whole during the winter they were marooned in the vicintiy of Donner Lake and also includes their various attempts at escape on their own and with rescuers--ed.

Illustrations in this reprint are from pre-1900 sources: *Oregon and California in 1848* (pp. 2, 18, 21, 37, 67, 96); *Beyond the Mississippi* (front cover)*; History of the Donner Party* (pp. 46, 56, 64, 76, 87). The back cover of Donner Lake is by Thomas Moran, from *Picturesque America.*

Copyright © 1996 VISTABOOKS
0637 Blue Ridge Rd., Silverthorne, CO 80498-8931.
ISBN 0-89646-037-1

Camp of Death:

The Donner Party Mountain Camp
1846 - 47

by J. Quinn Thornton

JOURNEY OF A PARTY OF CALIFORNIA EMIGRANTS IN 1846
FROM FORT BRIDGER TO THE SINKS OF OGDEN'S RIVER *

UPON my arrival at the town of San Francisco, I had the pleasure of receiving the friendly salutations and cordial greetings of many who had been my traveling companions in 1846. We had all commenced our journey together from the Wokaruska creek, west of the frontier settlements of Missouri, with my valued friend Col. Russell for our leader. In the divisions and subdivisions of the company which subsequently occurred, at the times and places noted in my journal, we were separated. Our respective companions, however, often traveled near to each other, and not unfrequently we encamped at the same grass and water. The reader, by turning back to my journal entries, under dates of July 21 and 22, 1846, will see that these California emigrants, at that time, determined upon following Lansford W. Hastings, upon a "cut-off" into California. This man had left California, and proceeded as far as the eastern side of the Rocky Mountains, and encamped at a place where the Sweet Water breaks through a cañon, at the point where the emigrants leave that river to enter the South Pass. He had come out for the purpose of inducing the emigrants to follow him through a "cut-off" into California. After meeting some of the advanced companies, and sending forward a messenger with a letter to those in the rear, informing them that he had explored a new and much better road into California than the old one, he returned to Fort Bridger, where he stated that he would remain until the California and Oregon emigrants should come up, when he would give a more particular description of his "cut-off."

The emigrants having all in time arrived at that place, Hastings assured them in the most solemn manner that the road over which he proposed to conduct them, was much nearer and better than the one via Fort Hall. He stated that there was an abundant supply of wood, water, and grass upon the whole line of the road, except one dry drive of thirty-five miles, or of forty at most; that they would have no difficult cañons to pass, and that the road was generally smooth, level, and hard.

* Ogden's River is now Humboldt River--ed.

Upon meeting in California many of those who survived the dangers of that disastrous cut-off, some of them expressed a wish that I would embody the facts, and publish them to the world in connection with my own journal, as constituting an important part of the history of the journey of the emigration of that year to the Pacific coast.

The notes from which I write the history of the journey of that party, after our final separation at Sandy, were written in the presence of Mr. Clarke of San Francisco, as the facts were verbally communicated to me by survivors.

It is proper to state, likewise, that such was the character of many of the shocking and heart-sickening scenes of the journey, that the emigrants had at first determined that they would, as far as practicable, keep these occurrences from the gaze of the world. But those who went from the settlements of California to the relief of the emigrants, at the Mountain Camp, necessarily obtained a knowledge of many facts. These were published, on their return, in the California Star, and also others that were materially erroneous. The latter class of newspaper notices, together with a multitude of floating rumors, finally led to the opinion that a circumstantial and plain narrative of the events referred to should be given to the world.

The California Company, after parting, on the 22d August, 1840,* at Sandy, from the company in which I traveled, proceeded on their road to Bridger's trading post, where they arrived July 25th. They left that place on the 28th, buoyant with hope, and filled with pleasing expectations of a speedy and happy termination of the toils and fatigues of travel. They continued traveling, without any circumstance of especial importance occurring, until August 3d, at which time a letter from Lansford W. Hastings was found by them, at the first crossing of Weber river, placed in the split of a stick, in such a situation as to call their attention to it. In this letter they were informed that the road down Weber river, over which the sixty-six wagons led by Lansford W. Hastings had passed, had been found to be a very bad one, and expressing fears that their sixty-six wagons could not be gotten through the cañon leading into the valley of the Great Salt Lake, then in sight; and advising them to remain in camp until he could return to them, for the purpose of showing them a better road than that through the cañon of Weber river which here breaks through the mountains. The company, piloted by Hastings, did with great difficulty succeed in passing. In this letter, Hastings had indicated another road which he affirmed was much better; and by pursuing which they would avoid the cañon. Messrs. Reed, Stanton, and Pike then went forward, for the purpose of exploring the contemplated new route.

*Thornton must have meant July, 1846—ed.

In eight days, Mr. Reed returned, reporting the practicability of the way, and that Messrs. Stanton and Pike were lost. These eight days thus spent materially contributed in bringing upon them the disasters which ensued. Upon receiving this report, they dispatched a party in search of Messrs. Stanton and Pike, and resumed their journey.

The company at that time consisted of the following persons: J. F. Reed, wife, and four children; George Donner, wife, and five children; Jacob Donner, wife, and seven children; Patrick Brinn,* wife and seven children; William Pike, wife and two children; William Foster, wife, and one child; Lewis Kiesburg, wife, and one child; Mrs. Murphy, a widow woman, and five children; William McCutcheon, wife, and one child; W. H. Eddy, wife, and two children; Noah James; Patrick Dolan; Samuel Shoemaker; John Denton; C. F. Stanton; Milton Elliot; _____ Smith; _____ Hardcoop; Joseph Rianhard; Augustus Spitzer; John Baptiste; _____ Antoine; _____ Herring; _____ Hallerin; Charles Burger; and Baylis Williams.

On the second day after resuming their journey they came to a grove of willows and quaking asp, through which their way led. Here they were compelled to open a road, which occupied one day. They again continued their journey, and passing over some very difficult bluffs, entered a hollow leading into the Utah River valley, and through which they were under the necessity of cutting eight miles of very thick timber and close-tangled underbrush. This difficult labor occupied eight days. On the sixth day of their being thus employed, Mr. W. Graves, wife, and eight children, and his son-in-law Jay Fosdick and wife, and John Snyder, came up with them. On the ninth day they left their encampment, and traveled into an opening which they supposed led out into the Utah River valley. Here Messrs. Stanton and Pike, who had been lost from the time Mr. Reed had gone forward with them to explore, were found by the party they had sent to hunt for them. These men reported the impracticability of passing down the valley in which they then were; and they advised their companions to pass over a low range of hills into a neighboring valley. This they did. Here they worked five days in cutting through the timber. On the seventh day they came out of the timber into a prairie, which led down to a cañon opening into the valley of the Utah. The cañon being impracticable as a wagon way, they doubled teams and got their wagons to the top of the hill, from which there was a gradual descent into the valley. They encamped in this; and resuming their journey on the next morning, struck the trail of the company in advance, at the crossing of the river which flows from the Utah Lake into the Great

---

*Patrick Breen in other accounts.

Salt Lake. They were thus occupied thirty days in traveling forty miles.

On September 3d, they again resumed their journey, pursuing their way around the south side of the Salt Lake, and along the trail of the company in advance.

The valley of the Utah river is about thirty-five miles long. One of the emigrants expressed to me the opinion, that as a happy abode for man, it surpassed in beauty, fertility, and every thing that can render a spot of earth desirable, any country that he had seen or expected to see. It is well supplied with streams of clear water, filled with salmon-trout. The atmosphere is remarkably pure and healthful, and the whole face of the country is covered with a heavy coat of the most nutritious grass. It is surrounded by high and rugged mountains, in the bosom of which it reposes in a calm and quiet beauty, that invites the weary and worn traveler to stay his wanderings and to enjoy, in the seclusion and loveliness of the scene, the happiness which he has sought in vain amidst the crowded marts of commerce or the fashion and dissipation of cities. The peaceful stillness and loveliness of this most interesting valley, and the happiness to which it seemed to invite, strangely contrasted with the suffering of body and the anguish of spirit which that devoted party subsequently endured.

In listening to the description of this valley, as thus substantially given to me by the emigrants, I was strongly reminded of my own emotions and feelings when, after passing over a long and cheerless waste, I suddenly emerged from sands and artemisia into a beautiful little valley of bubbling springs, and verdure, and flowers. At such a time, it has appeared far more interesting and lovely, from the striking contrast, than it would have done, had I met with it in a country of general fertility. On these occasions I have often experienced a cloud of sadness to come over my spirit, as I reflected that the leaves around me must wither, and the flowers, that modestly turned up their beautiful faces to the sun, must fall silently and unobserved. The beauty of the place, the penciling of the leaves, the sparkling of the fountains, the rippling of the streams, and the whole aspect of the surrounding scenery of nature rejoicing in her beauty, yet induced within my mind saddened emotions, as I reflected how evanescent were all these varied expressions of the beautiful and the real. The interest I have thus felt in all this, was but a tribute of grief and affection, eminently befitting and proper in one whom Nature had never deserted in adversity, but had a thousand times whispered in his ear the promise of a new and better condition of being, in a world not subjected to the decree of the fell destroyer, where the fields are ever fresh and verdant, and the flowers never fade.

It is in this valley that the Mormons have made a settlement and laid out a town, about four miles above the emigrant road.

The Mormons, upon being expelled from Nauvoo, in 1846, made a large settlement at Council Bluffs, upon the Missouri river. This is designed rather for a place of outfit and preparation for the journey across the Rocky Mountains, than as a permanent settlement. A party, consisting of about three hundred and fifty, left Council Bluffs very early in the year 1847, for the purpose of exploring the Salt Lake country. In June they were followed by about fifteen hundred souls, with provisions and supplies for eighteen months. They purpose to plant and sow crops for 1848; and if the climate and soil should be found favorable to the plan of making a permanent settlement at this place, they will establish one here, for the purpose of making it a half-way or stopping place for persons traveling from the Atlantic to the Pacific. Many thousands are expected, during each succeeding year, to settle at this point.

So soon as a settlement shall be established at this place, they propose to explore the mountains, for the purpose of obtaining minerals. They also contemplate opening a new road from the Salt Lake into California. They measured the distance from the Council Bluffs to the Salt Lake, and found it to be eleven hundred miles. The distance from the Salt Lake to San Francisco, now estimated at seven hundred miles, they believe can be diminished to five hundred.

On the evening of September 3d, the emigrants encamped on the southeast side of the Great Salt Lake. On the morning of the next day, they resumed their journey, and at about 9 o'clock commenced passing round the point of a mountain which here runs down to the beach of the lake. This occupied the entire day. Here Mr. Reed broke an axletree, and they had to go a distance of fifteen miles to obtain timber to repair it. By working all night, Mr. Eddy and Samuel Shoemaker completed the repair for Mr. Reed. About 4 o'clock, P.M., Mr. Hallerin, from St. Joseph, died of consumption, in Mr. George Donner's wagon. About 8 o'clock, this wagon (which had stopped) came up, with the dead body of their fellow-traveler. He died in the exercise of a humble trust and confidence in the ability and willingness of the blessed Redeemer to save his soul. The melancholy event filled all hearts with sadness, and with feelings of solemnity, they committed his body to its silent and lonely grave in the wilderness. Nor did they seek to disguise the tears that silently coursed down many a care-worn face, as they took their last adieu of the lost fellow-traveler. The day of the 5th was spent, with the exception of a change of camp, in committing the body of their friend to the dust. They buried him at the side of an emigrant who had died in the advance company. The deceased gave his property, some $1500, to Mr. George Donner.

On September 6th, they resumed their journey, and after dark encamped at a place to which they gave the name of the Twenty Wells. The name was suggested by the circumstance of there being at this place that number of natural wells, filled to the very surface of the earth with the purest cold water. They sounded some of them with lines of more than seventy feet, without finding bottom. They varied from six inches to nine feet in diameter. None of them overflowed; and, what is most extraordinary, the ground was dry and hard near the very edge of the water, and upon taking water out, the wells would instantly fill again.

On the morning of the 7th, they left camp; and after making a long and hard drive, encamped in a large and beautiful meadow, abundantly supplied with the very best grass. Here they found a number of wells, differing in no respect from those just mentioned. Here they found a letter from Lansford W. Hastings, informing them that it would occupy two days and nights of hard driving to reach the next water and grass. They consequently remained in camp on the 8th, to rest and recruit their cattle. Having done this, and cut grass to carry on the way, they resumed their journey at daylight on the morning of September 9th, with many apprehensions, and at about ten o'clock A.M., of the 12th, Mr. Eddy and some others succeeded, after leaving his wagons twenty miles back, in getting his team across the Great Salt Plain, to a beautiful spring at the foot of a mountain on the west side of the plain, and distant eighty miles from their camp of the 7th and 8th. On the evening of the 12th, just at dark, Mr. Reed came up to them, and informed them that his wagons and those of the Messrs. Donner had been left about forty miles in the rear, and that the drivers were trying to bring the cattle forward to the water. After remaining about an hour, he started back to meet the drivers with the cattle, and to get his family. Mr. Eddy accompanied him back five miles, with a bucket of water for an ox of his that had become exhausted, in consequence of thirst, and had lain down. Mr. Reed met the drivers ten miles from the spring, coming forward with the cattle. He continued on, and the drivers came into camp about midnight, having lost all of Mr. Reed's team after passing him. The Messrs. Donner got to water, with a part of their teams, at about 2 o'clock, A.M., of September 13th. Mr. Eddy started back at daylight on the morning of the 13th, and at dawn of day on the 14th, he brought up Mrs. Reed and children, and his wagon. On the afternoon of the 14th, they started back with Mr. Reed and Mr. Graves, for the wagons of the Messrs. Donner and Reed; and brought them up with horses and mules, on the evening of the 15th.

It is impossible to describe the dismay and anguish with which that perilous and exhausting drive filled the stoutest hearts. Many families were completely ruined. They were yet in a country of hostile Indians, far from all succor, betrayed by one of their own countrymen. They could not tell what was the character of the road yet before them, since the man in whose veracity they reposed confidence, had proved himself so utterly unworthy of it. To retreat across the desert to Bridger was impossible. There was no way left to them, but to advance; and this they now regarded as perilous in the extreme. The cattle that survived were exhausted and broken down; but to remain there was to die. Feeble and dispirited, therefore, they slowly resumed their journey.

On this drive thirty-six head of working cattle were lost, and the oxen that survived were greatly injured. One of Mr. Reed's wagons was brought to camp; and two, with all they contained, were buried in the plain. George Donner lost one wagon. Kiesburg also lost a wagon. The atmosphere was so dry upon the plain, that the wood-work of all the wagons shrank to a degree that made it next to impossible to get any of them through.

The name of this place indicates its character in some respects, and I need not now detain the reader with a description of it; but I can not forbear mentioning an extraordinary optical illusion related to me by one of the emigrants. They saw themselves, their wagons, their teams, and the dogs with them, in very many places, while crossing this plain, repeated many times in all the distinctness and vividness of life. Mr. Eddy informed me that he was surprised to see twenty men all walking in the same direction in which he was traveling. They all stopped at the same time, and the motions of their bodies corresponded. At length he was astounded with the discovery that they were men whose features and dress were like his own, and that they were imitating his own motions. When he stood still, they stood still, and when he advanced, they did so also. In short, they were living and moving images of himself, and of his actions. Subsequently he saw the caravan repeated in the same extraordinary and startling manner.

Mr. Eddy having ascended the side of the mountain that commanded a view of the plain below, saw the morning spread out upon the hills, and, at length, beheld the sun arise above the plain, and cover it with splendor and glory. The mind can not conceive, much less the tongue express, the ravishing beauty of the scene that instantly kindled into a magnificence, grandeur, and loveliness unequaled — cloud-formed masses of purple ranges, bordered with the most brilliant gold, lay piled above the eastern mountains. Peaks were seen shooting up into narrow lines of crimson drapery, and festooning of greenish orange, the whole being covered with a blue sky of singular beauty and transparency. All the colors of the prism bordered the country before him, and ten thousand hues of heavenly radiance spread and diffused themselves over it, as the sun continued to ascend. The king of day seemed to rise from his throne, and cast upon his footstool his gorgeous robes of light, sparkling with unnumbered gems. Here nature appeared to have collected all her glittering beauties together in one chosen place.

Having yoked some loose cows, as a team for Mr. Reed, they broke up their camp on the morning of September 16th, and resumed their toilsome journey, with feelings which can be appreciated by those only who have traveled the road under somewhat similar circumstances. On this day they traveled six miles, encountering a very severe snow storm. About 3 o'clock, P.M., they met Milton Elliot and William Graves, returning from a fruitless effort to find some cattle that had got off. They informed them that they were then in the immediate vicinity of a spring, at which commenced another dry drive of forty miles. They encamped for the night, and at dawn of day of September 17th, they resumed their journey, and at 4 o'clock, A.M., of the 18th they arrived at water and grass, some of their cattle having perished, and the teams which survived being in a very enfeebled condition. Here the most of the little property which Mr. Reed still had, was buried, or *cached*, together with that of others. As the term *cache* will frequently occur, I ought to remark that it is used for what is hidden. *Cacher*, the verb, is equivalent to *to conceal*. Here, Mr. Eddy, proposed putting his team to Mr. Reed's wagon, and letting Mr. Pike have his wagon, so that the three families could be taken on. This was done. They remained in camp during the day of the 18th to complete these arrangements, and to recruit their exhausted cattle.

What is the cause of the sterility and aridness of this region, and also of much of the country between the Mississippi and Middle Oregon, is a question that will never, perhaps, be fully answered. It is a remarkable fact, however, that all such districts of country are destitute of timber. And Humboldt has almost demonstrated that the streams of a country fail in proportion to the destruction of timber. If the streams fail the seasons will continue to be worse, because of their becoming each year more dry. It has been observed by the old settlers of a country, that water-courses have failed as the forests have been cleared away. Humboldt, in speaking of the valley of Aragu, in Venezuela says that the lake receded as agriculture advanced, until fine plantations were established on its banks. The desolating wars that swept over the country after the separation of the province from Spain, arrested the process of clearing. The trees again grew up, with a rapidity known only to the tropics, and the waters of the lake again rose, and inundated the low plantations.

Early on the morning of Sept. 19th, the emigrants broke up their encampment, and passing over a low range of mountains, came down into the head of a most beautiful and fertile valley, well supplied with water and grass. They encamped on the west side of this valley. They gave to it the name of the Valley of the Fifty Springs, the name being suggested by that number being here found. They encamped by one of them, situated in the centre of a cone about ten feet high. The water rose to the top, but did not flow over. Many of the springs were hot, some warm, and many cool, and slightly acid. They saw hundreds of Indians, who were friendly, and seemed never before to have seen a white man. Here were great numbers of antelopes and Rocky Mountain sheep, which they had no difficulty in killing. This valley is destitute of timber, and is about fifteen miles wide.

Early on the morning of the 20th, they continued their journey, and traveling about fifteen miles down the valley in a southerly direction, encamped at night near good grass and water. They proceeded down this valley three days, making about fifty miles of travel. The valley, however, still continued to extend south, beyond the reach of their vision, and presenting the same general appearance.

On the morning of Sept. 23d, they left the valley of the Fifty Springs, and crossing over a low range of mountains, came into a valley of great beauty and fertility. Crossing this valley, which was here seven miles wide, and finding water, they again encamped. In all these valleys, there are no springs on their eastern sides. The water being uniformly found breaking out at the foot of the mountains, upon the western side.

They had been traveling in a southerly direction for many days, but on the morning of the 24th, they commenced traveling due north. This they continued to do three days, following the tracks of the wagons in advance. They then turned a little west of north, and traveled two days, so that in nine days' travel they made but about thirty miles westward.

On the night of the 28th, they encamped at the head of a cañon leading into the valley of Mary's or Ogden's river. Here they saw large bodies of Indians in a state of perfect nudity. They hovered around in the vicinity, but did not come into camp.

On the morning of the 29th, they entered the cañon, and traveling about eight miles, found, at 11 o'clock, P.M., a place sufficiently large to admit of an encampment out of the water.

On the 20th, they pursued their way down the cañon, and after traveling eight miles, came out into the valley of Mary's river, at night, and encamped on the bank of the stream, having struck the road leading from Fort Hall. Here some Indians came to camp, and informed them by signs, that they were yet distant about two hundred miles from the sinks of that river.

Journey of the California Emigrants from Ogden's River to the East Side of the Sierra Nevada

On the morning of October 1st, they resumed their journey, and traveled along the usual route down Ogden's river, and encamped that evening at some hot springs, at the foot of a high range of hills.

On the morning of the 2d, they commenced passing over these hills. About 11 o'clock, an Indian, who spoke a little English, came to them, to whom they gave the name of Thursday, on account of their believing that to be the day; although at the time, they were inclined to believe that they had lost one day in their calculation of time. About 4 o'clock, P.M., another came to them, who also spoke a little English. He frequently used the words "jee," "who," and "huoy;" thereby showing that he had been with previous emigrants. They traveled all that day, and at dark encamped at a spring about half way down the side of the mountain. A fire broke out in the grass, soon after the camp fires had been kindled, which would have consumed three of the wagons, but for the assistance of these two Indians. The Indians were fed, and after the evening meal they lay down by one of the fires, but rose in the night, stealing a fine shirt and a yoke of oxen from Mr. Graves.

On the evening of October 5th, the emigrants again encamped on Ogden's river, after a hard and exhausting drive. During the night the Indians stole a horse from Mr. Graves.

On the morning of October 5th, they broke up their camp, and the caravan proceeded on its way. Mr. Eddy went out hunting antelope, and spent the forenoon in this manner, being frequently shot at by the Indians. At noon he came up with the company, which had stopped to take some refreshments, at the foot of a very high and long sand-hill, covered with rocks at the top. At length they commenced ascending the hill. All the wagons had been taken up but Mr. Reed's, Mr. Pike's, and one of Mr. Graves', the latter driven by John Snyder. Milton Elliot, who was Mr. Reed's driver, took Mr. Eddy's team, which was on Mr. Reed's wagon, and joined it to Mr. Pike's team. The cattle of this team, being unruly, became entangled with that of Mr. Graves', driven by Snyder; and a quarrel ensued between him and Elliot. Snyder at length commenced quarreling with Mr. Reed, and made some threats of whipping him, which threats he seemed about to attempt executing. Mr. Reed then drew a knife, without, however, attempting to use it, and told Snyder that he did not wish to have any difficulty with him. Snyder told him that he would whip him, "any how;" and turning the butt of his whip, gave Mr. Reed a severe blow upon the head, which cut it very much. As Reed was in the act of dodging the blow, he stabbed Snyder a little below the collar-bone, cutting off the first rib, and driving the knife through the left lung. Snyder after this struck Mrs. Reed a blow upon the head, and Mr. Reed two blows upon the head, the last one bringing him down upon his knees. Snyder expired in about fifteen minutes. Mr. Reed, although the blood was running down over his face and shoulders from his own wounds, manifested the greatest anguish of spirit, and threw the knife away from him into the river. Although Mr. Reed was thus compelled to do as he did, the occurrence produced much feeling against him; and in the evening Kiesburg proposed to hang him. To this, however, he was probably prompted by a feeling of resentment, produced by Mr. Reed having been mainly instrumental in his expulsion from one of the companies, while on the South Platte, for grossly improper conduct. Mr. Eddy had two six-shooters, two double-barreled pistols, and a rifle; Milton Elliot had one rifle, and a double-barreled shot gun; and Mr. Reed had one six-shooter, and a brace of double-barreled pistols, and rifle. Thus Mr. Reed's comrades were situated, and they determined that he should not die. Mr. Eddy, however, proposed that Mr. Reed should leave the camp. This was finally agreed to, and he accordingly left the next morning; not, however, before he had assisted in committing to the grave the body of the unhappy young man.

On the morning of October 6th, they quitted the wretched scene of mortal strife, and in the evening encamped on Ogden's river.

Leaving camp on the morning of the 7th, they proceeded on until about eleven o'clock, when they found a letter from Mr. Reed, informing them of a battle between one of the advanced companies and the Indians. On the forenoon of this day, a number of arrows were shot at Mr. Eddy and Mr. Pike, while out hunting for game, which the reduced amount of their provisions had by this time made it necessary to seek. Upon arriving at their evening encampment, they found that Hardcoop, a Belgian, who had given out, and had been carried in Kiesburg's wagon for several days, was missing. Kiesburg professed not to know what had become of him, but suspecting that there was some wrong committed, a man was sent back upon a horse, for the old man. He was found about five miles in the rear. Hardcoop stated that Kiesburg had put him out of the wagon to perish.

On the morning of Oct. 8, they *cached* a part of Mr. Eddy's tools and clothing, and Mr. Reed's wagon, and procured a lighter wagon of Mr. Graves. At about nine o'clock they started. In about half an hour Hardcoop came to Mr. Eddy, and informed him that Kiesburg had again put him out of the wagon — that he was an old man, being more than sixty years of age, and in addition to the infirmities usually attendant upon one of his advanced years, was sick and worn down by the toils and hardships of the way; and he concluded by requesting Mr. Eddy to carry him in his wagon, as it was utterly impossible for him to travel on foot. Mr. Eddy replied that they were then in the sand, and if he could in some way get forward until they got out, he would do what he could. He told me that he shuddered at the thought of seeing him left to perish by the way; and that he knew that the picture of his bones bleaching in the wilderness would haunt his memory to the latest day of his life. Hardcoop replied that he would make an effort. The emigrants traveled on until night. As soon as they got into camp, inquiry was made for Hardcoop. Some boys who had been driving cattle stated that they had seen him last sitting under a large bush of sage, or artemisia, exhausted and completely worn out. At this time his feet had swollen until they burst. Mr. Eddy, having the guard during the fore part of the night, built a large fire on the side of the hill, to guide Hardcoop to the camp, if it was possible for him to come up. Milton Elliot had the guard during the latter part of the night, and he kept up the fire for the same purpose. The night was very cold; but when morning dawned, the unhappy Hardcoop did not come up. Mrs. Reed, Milton Elliot, and Mr. Eddy then went to Kiesburg, and besought him to return for the old man. This, Kiesburg, in a very heartless and inhuman manner, refused to do. No other persons, excepting Patrick Brinn and Mr. Graves having horses, upon which he could be carried, they then applied to Patrick Brinn, who replied that it was impossible, and that he must perish. Application was then made to Graves, who said that he would not kill his horses to save the life of Hardcoop, and that he might die; and, in great anger, requested that he might not be troubled any more upon the subject. Milton Elliot, William Pike, and Mr. Eddy then proposed to go back on foot and carry him up, but the company refused to wait. Being in an Indian country, they were compelled to go forward with their traveling companions. They arrived at the place where Applegate's cut-off leaves the Ogden's river road, about 11 o'clock, A.M., of this day (Oct. 9); and having halted for the purpose of resting and taking a little refreshment, they again sought to induce Brinn and Graves to let them have horses to go back for the unfortunate Hardcoop; the proposal was again violently re-pulsed. Thus disappointed and defeated in every effort, they were, at last, under the dreadful necessity of relinquishing every hope, and of leaving their aged and exhausted fellow-traveler to die a most miserable death. He was from Antwerp, in Belgium — was a cutler by trade, and had a son and daughter in his native city. He had come to the United States for the purpose of seeing the country. He owned a farm near Cincinnati, Ohio, and intended, after visiting California, to go back to Ohio, sell his farm, and return to Antwerp, for the purpose of spending with his children the evening of his days.

Proceeding from their 11 o'clock halt, they arrived at a bed of deep, loose sand about 4 o'clock, P.M., and did not succeed in crossing it until 4 o'clock in the morning of Oct. 10, when they halted upon the place where Mr. Salle, who had been killed by the Indians, had been buried. His body had been dug up by the savages, and his bones, which had been picked by wolves, were bleaching in the sun. Here they *cached* another wagon, and at this place all of Graves' horses were stolen. At 10 o'clock they drove on, and encamped at night on Ogden's river, with scarcely any grass for their cattle, the water being very bad.

On the morning of the 11th George Donner, Jacob Donner, and Wolfinger lost eighteen head of cattle. Graves, also, had a cow stolen by Indians. They encamped on the night of the 11th on a small spot of very poor grass. The water here, also, was deficient in quantity and bad in quality. Brinn had a fine mare die in the mud. He asked Mr. Eddy to help him to get her out. Mr. Eddy referred him to poor Hardcoop, and refused. Several cattle had arrows shot at them during the night, but none of them died in consequence.

On the morning of Oct. 12, the emigrants resumed their journey. One of Mr. Eddy's oxen gave out during the day, and they left him. At 12 o'clock at night they encamped at the sinks of Ogden's river. At daylight on the morning of the 13th they drove their cattle to grass, and put them under a guard. The guard came in to breakfast, and in their absence the Indians killed twenty-one head, including the whole of Mr. Eddy's team, except one ox; and the whole of Wolfinger's, except one. Wolfinger wished to *cache* his goods at the sinks, but the company refused to wait. Rianhard and Spitzer, who were traveling with him, remained behind to assist him. Three days afterward the two former came up to the company at Truckee river, and said that the Indians came down from the hills upon them, and after killing Wolfinger, drove them from the wagons, which they burned, after taking the goods out. Wolfinger had a considerable amount of money. I was informed by Mr. Eddy that George Donner, with whom Rianhard subsequently traveled, told him that Wolfinger had not died as stated — that this fact he learned from a confession made by Rianhard a short time previous to his death; and that he would make the facts public as soon as he arrived in the settlements. Donner having perished, nothing further was ever known of the matter.

In mentioning these facts I am aware that I am anticipating some of the events of this narrative, and I will only remark that Donner, Rianhard, and Spitzer having all been subsequently starved to death, it is probable the facts will never be revealed.

Here Mr. Eddy *cached* every thing he had, except the clothing which he and his family had on. On this morning they partook of their last remaining mouthful of food. The Indians were upon the adjacent hills, looking down upon them, and absolutely laughing at their calamity. The lock of Mr. Eddy's rifle had been broken some days before, and the gun left. He could not obtain one, and had he been able to do so, it would have been worse than insanity for him to have encountered the Indians alone. Dejected and sullen, he took up about three pounds of loaf sugar, put some bullets in his pocket, and stringing his powderhorn upon his shoulders, took up his boy in his arms while his afflicted Eleanor carried their still more helpless infant, and in this most miserable and forlorn plight, they set out once more on foot to make their way through the pitiless wilderness. Trackless, snowclad mountains intercepted their progress, and seemed to present an impassable barrier to all human succor: — mountains, the passage of which, with even the accessories of emigrant wagons, and in the most pleasant season, would have been a feat of no small difficulty. Without shoes— these having been worn out by the jagged rocks—they had nothing to protect their feet but moccasins, which were also so much worn as to be of little service. Their painful and perilous way led over broken rocks, presenting acute angles, or prickly pears, which alike lacerated their feet in the most dreadful manner. Nature disputed their passage, and Heaven seemed to be offended. They struggled on, however, with their precious charge, without food or water, until 4 o'clock on the morning of the 14th, when they arrived at a spring that jetted up a column of boiling hot water, about twenty feet high. It was situated in a region that had been rent into millions of fragments by volcanic fires. The desolation was such as to impress upon the mind the idea of expiring nature convulsed with the throes and agonies of the last great and terrible day, or of an angry Deity having taken vengeance upon a guilty world. Having obtained some coffee from Mrs. Donner, Mr. Eddy put it into a pot, and thus boiled it in the hot spring for the nourishment of his wife and children, refusing to partake of it himself. He told me that he should never forget the inexpressible emotions he felt on seeing them thus revive. Under such circumstances of extreme privation, how much more forcibly does the wasteful prodigality of the rich appear. Although he had suffered the loss of all he possessed, yet had it pleased Heaven to have spared him one blow, he might have still been comparatively happy. But God, who is ever wise and just in the allotments of his providence, had decreed otherwise.

About 9 o'clock the party left the Geyser Spring and traveled all that day until sunset, over a road in no respect different from that of the 13th. At this time Mr. Eddy's children were in great danger of perishing for the want of water. He applied to Patrick Brinn, who he knew had ten gallons, for a half pint to give to them. Brinn denied having any; but this Mr. Eddy knew to be untrue, for he had himself filled Brinn's cask at the sinks of Ogden's river; Brinn finally admitted that he had water, but said he did not know how far water was yet distant from them, and he feared that his own family would require it. Mr. Eddy told him, with an energy he never before felt, that he would have it or have Brinn's life. He immediately turned away from Brinn, and went in quest of the water, and gave some to his children.

At sunset they arrived at an exceedingly difficult sand-ridge of ten miles in width. They crossed it about 4 o'clock on the morning of the 15th, the company losing three yoke of cattle that died from fatigue.

Neither Mr. Eddy nor his wife had tasted food for two days and nights, nor had the children any thing except the sugar with which he left the sinks [of] Ogden's river. He applied to Mrs. Graves and Mrs. Brinn for a small piece of meat for his wife and children, who were very faint. They both refused. The emigrants remained in camp to rest the cattle. The Indians killed some of them during the day.

Mr. Eddy procured a gun in the morning, and started to kill some geese which he heard. In about two hours he returned with nine very fat ones. Mrs. Brinn and Mrs. Graves congratulated him, and expressed the opinion that they were very fine, and wondered what he would do with them. He invited them to help themselves, and they each took two. He gave Kiesburg one.

Oct. 16th, early in the morning, they resumed their journey, and commenced driving up Truckee river. Nothing of importance occurred until Oct. 19th, about 10 o'clock, A.M., when they met Mr. C. F. Stanton and two Indian *vaqueros* (cow-herds) of Capt. Sutter, one named Lewis, and the other Salvadore. Mr. Stanton had flour and a little dried meat, which he had procured for them. I omitted to state that on the day they broke up their encampment on the Salt Lake, they dispatched Messrs. Stanton and McCutcheon to go to Capt. Sutter's Fort for relief. They drove on during the day, and Mr. Stanton and the *vaqueros* continued on to some of the families one day in the rear.

October 20—On this day Wm. Pike was killed by the accidental discharge of a six-shooter in the hands of Wm. Foster. He died in one hour: he was shot through in the back.

On the evening of October 22d, they crossed the Truckee river, the forty-ninth and last time, in eighty miles. They encamped on the top of a hill. Here nineteen oxen were shot by an Indian, who put one arrow in each ox. The cattle did not die. Mr. Eddy caught him in the act, and fired upon him as he fled. The ball struck him between the shoulders, and came out at the breast. At the crack of the rifle he sprung up about three feet, and with a terrible yell fell down a bank into a bunch of willows.

On the morning of October 23d they resumed their journey, and continued traveling without any thing of importance occurring until October 28th at dark, when they encamped upon Truckee Lake,* situated at the foot of Fremont's Pass* of the main chain of the Sierra Nevada. The Pass is here 9838 feet high.

On the morning of Oct. 29th, they again continued their journey, and went on within three miles of the top of the Pass, where they found the snow about five feet deep. This compelled them to return to a cabin, which was situated one mile in advance of their camp of the previous night. Here they remained in camp during the 30th. At dark their fellow-travelers, Stanton, Graves, the Donners, and some others, came up.

On the morning of Oct. 31st the whole body again started to cross the mountain. They succeeded in getting within three miles of the top of the Pass. The snow had deepened to about ten feet. The night was bitterly cold; the wind howled through the trees, and the snow and hail descended. Finding it utterly impossible to cross, they commenced retracing their steps on the morning of November 1st, and arrived at the cabin about 4 o'clock.

MR. EDDY AND FAMILY SETTING OUT.

*Now Donner Lake and Donner Pass. The elevation of Donner Lake is 5933 feet, and of Donner Pass, 7189 feet.

The Mountain Camp

THEY now saw that it would be necessary to winter here. On the morning of November 2d, Mr. Eddy commenced building a cabin. When finished, the following day, he went into it, with Mrs. Murphy and family, and Wm. Foster and family, Nov. 3d. The snow at the place at which they were encamped, was about one foot deep. A single ox constituted the whole stock upon which the family were to winter.

Mr. Eddy commenced hunting on the 4th, and succeeded in killing a prairie wolf, of which supper was made in the evening for all in the cabin. On the 5th he succeeded in killing an owl, of which supper was made. The Messrs. Graves, Donner, Dolan, and Brinn commenced killing their cattle. Mr. Eddy also killed his ox. On the 6th, an ox belonging to Graves starved to death. He refused to save it for meat, but upon Mr. Eddy's applying to him for it, he would not let him have it for less than $25. This, Mr. Eddy told me, he had paid to the estate of the deceased Graves since getting into the settlement. Mr. Eddy spent the 7th in hunting, but returned at night with a sad and desponding heart, without any game. The three following days he assisted Graves in putting up a cabin for himself and family, and Mrs. Reed and her family. The day after, they cooked some of their poor beef.

On the 12th, Mr. Eddy, C. T. Stanton, Wm. Graves, Sen., Jay Fosdick, James Smith, Charles Burger, Wm. Foster, Antoine (a Spaniard), John Baptiste, Lewis, Salvadore, Augustus Spitzer, Mary Graves, Sarah Fosdick, and Milton Elliot, being the strongest of the party, started to cross the mountains on foot. Mr. Eddy, in narrating the afflicting story, said to me, that he could never forget the parting scene between himself and family; but he hoped to get in and obtain relief, and return with the means for their rescue. They started with a small piece of beef each; but they had scarcely gone within three miles of the top of the Pass, when the snow, which was soft, and about ten feet deep, compelled them again to return to the cabins, which they reached about midnight.

Nov. 13th, Mr. Eddy succeeded in killing two ducks, but no one would let him have a gun without he gave them half he killed. The next day, very faint from want of food, he resumed his hunting, and at length came upon an enormously large grisly-bear track. Under other circumstances, he would have preferred seeing the tracks of one to seeing the animal itself. But now, weak and faint as he was, he was eager to come up with it. So fierce and powerful is this animal, and so great is its tenacity of life, that the Indians almost uniformly avoid it. Even the most daring and successful white hunters who are acquainted with its habits, usually decline shooting at it, unless they are in a position that enables them to spring up into a tree in the event of the first shot failing to bring it down. This very seldom happens, unless the shot takes effect in the brain. Lewis and Clarke give an account of a bear killed by their party, which was not brought down until it had received five wounds, any one of which would have immediately disabled any other animal. Even then, one of their number very narrowly escaped with his life by leaping down a precipice and plunging into the river. It invariably attacks all persons whom it suddenly finds near it. If it be distant, a noise will cause it to run away; but even in this case it uniformly makes battle if wounded. With a full knowledge of its real character, and although he had heard the stories of many exciting adventures, which were not the less interesting because some of them were unreasonable, and others even impossible, yet he now was exceedingly desirous of coming up with an animal he would otherwise have been most careful to shun. He was not long in finding the object of his search. At the distance of about ninety yards he saw the bear, with its head to the ground, engaged in digging roots. The beast was in a small skirt of prairie, and Mr. Eddy, taking advantage of a large firtree near which he was at the moment, kept himself in concealment. Having put into his mouth the only bullet that was not in his gun, so that he might quickly reload in case of an emergency, he deliberately fired. The bear immediately reared upon its hind feet, and seeing the smoke from Mr. Eddy's gun, ran fiercely toward him, with open jaws. By the time the gun was reloaded, the bear had reached the tree, and, with a fierce growl, pursued Mr. Eddy round it, who, running swifter than the animal, came up with it in the rear, and disabled it by a shot in the shoulder, so that it was no longer able to pursue him. He then dispatched the bear by knocking it on the head with a club. Upon examination, he found that the first shot had pierced its heart. He then returned to the Mountain Camp for assistance to bring in his prize.

Graves and Eddy went out after the bear. On the way out Graves said that he believed he should perish in the mountain; that he feared that the judgment of God would come upon him, for not

KILLING THE BEAR.

assisting Hardcoop up to the wagon, when Kiesburg put him out, and for driving Mr. Reed out of camp. They, however, finally contrived to get in the bear after dark. Mr. Eddy gave one half to Mr. Foster for the use of the gun. A part of it was likewise given to Mr. Graves and to Mrs. Reed. The bear weighed about 800 lbs.

Nov. 15th, Mr. Eddy killed a duck and one gray squirrel. Nothing of importance occurred between this date and the 21st, beyond the fears of starvation, and the increasing weakness of the emigrants. On this day, six women and sixteen men, including Stanton and the two Indians, made another effort to cross the mountain on foot. The morning was fine; the wind from the northwest. They crossed the pass on the crust of the snow. Mr. Eddy measured the snow here, and found it to be twenty-five feet deep. They encamped in a little valley on the west side of the mountain, in six feet snow. They experienced great difficulty in kindling a fire and in getting wood, in consequence of their extreme weakness. Here Mr. Stanton and the two Indian boys refused to go any further, in consequence of not being able to get along with seven mules belonging to Capt. Sutter. Fully aware of their peril, Mr. Eddy exhausted all his reasoning powers in a vain effort to induce them to proceed; urging the imminent danger of their all perishing from starvation, and offering to become responsible for the mules. He knew that Capt. Sutter would rather lose the animals, than know that his fellow-beings had perished in a foolish attempt to save them: but all persuasion was in vain. He then proposed that they should compel the Indians to go forward. This was objected to; and a good deal of angry feeling was exhibited by Mr. Eddy, and those against whose plans he vainly remonstrated. Accordingly, on the morning of the 22d, faint and dispirited, they again commenced their return to their unhappy companions in peril. They arrived, almost exhausted, at the cabins about midnight. The previous night had been most bitterly cold; but the weather of this day was clear, and the sun shone brightly upon the snow.

The subsequent day the weather was clear, and the wind westerly. Mrs. Eddy and her children were very weak, but exhibited great courage and fortitude.

The weather on the 25th was very cloudy, and there was every appearance of another snow-storm. The previous night had been intensely cold. They proposed to make another effort the next day, if the weather would admit of it; but the snow began to descend on the afternoon of the 25th, in great flakes, and so thick that it was impossible to see beyond a few feet. This continued with greater or less violence, and with but occasional intermissions, until the 29th, when it ceased for a few hours. The wind changed from northwest to west. By this time it was three feet deep in the valley, which made it very difficult, in their feeble condition, for the emigrants to get wood. On this day Patrick Brinn sold William Foster a yoke of oxen, taking a gold watch and some other property in security, and then killed the last ox he had. On the 30th it snowed very heavily, and there was every appearance of its continuing. It was next to impossible for any living thing without wings to get out.

December 1.—The snow continued to fall as when it first commenced, and upon being measured was found to be from six to six and a half feet deep. The wind blew in fearful and terrific blasts from the west. The cold was intense: the wretched sojourners were nearly naked, and almost without food: the snow had now become so deep as to make it increasingly difficult to get wood for fuel. They were completely housed up, and were cut off from all the world, and sympathies of life. The few cattle that had lived up to this time, and the horses, and Capt. Sutter's mules, were all supposed to be lost in the snow, and none now cherished the least hope of ever finding them.

The snow ceased falling on the 3d; and although the weather continued cloudy all day, the atmosphere was sufficiently warm to thaw the snow a little. They measured the snow on the 5th, and found it seven or eight feet deep. The sun shone again, clear and beautiful, causing every thing, after the long and terrific storm, to assume its wonted aspect. The cheering light once more rekindled hope in the hearts of the desolate travelers.

The morning of the 6th opened upon them fine and clear; and Messrs. Stanton and Graves spent the day in manufacturing snow-shoes, preparatory to making another effort to cross the mountains. Nothing had been heard from the mules, and all, now, at least, saw that they ought to have been killed for food, as Mr. Eddy proposed at the camp on the 22d, after their return from the mountain. Then Graves and others objected, fearing that it might be necessary to pay for them. The morning of the 8th was fine and clear, although the previous night had been distressingly cold. They found it very difficult to obtain enough wood to cook their now nearly putrid beef, or even to keep them warm. The wind, during the day, was from the southwest.

About 11 o'clock, A.M., Dec. 9, the wind commenced blowing from the northwest, and their hearts almost died within them, as they again saw the snow beginning to descend. Mr. Stanton sought to obtain some food for himself and the two Indians, Lewis and Salvadore, but did not obtain much. Patrick Brinn, on the day before this, took Spitzer into his cabin in a state so weak from starvation, that he could not rise without help. The snow continued to fall on the 10th. On the 13th, it fell faster than on any previous day; and in a short time was eight feet on a level. The prospect became every moment more appalling. Death seemed inevitably to be awaiting them. Messrs. Eddy, Stanton, Graves, and others spent the day in preparing to make another attempt to cross the mountains. On the 14th Baylis Williams died of starvation. He was the first victim of this hapless company who thus expired, and their feelings and reflections may, perhaps, be imagined, but can not be described.

JOURNEY OF A PARTY FROM THE MOUNTAIN CAMP INTO THE SETTLEMENTS OF CALIFORNIA

ON the 16th of December, the following persons started on snow-shoes to cross the mountains: — Sarah Fosdick, Mary Graves, William Foster, Sarah Foster, C. T. Stanton, William Graves, Jay Fosdick, Wm. Murphy, Charles Burger, Harriet Pike, Lemuel Murphy, Patrick Dolan, Antoine, Lewis, Salvadore, Mrs. McCutcheon, and William Eddy.

The night previous to their departure was exceedingly cold. Their friends were in a state of extreme suffering and want. The hollow cheek, the wasted form, and the deep sunken eye of his wife, Mr. Eddy told me he should never forget. "Oh," said he, "the bitter anguish of my wrung and agonized spirit, when I turned away from her; and yet no tear would flow to relieve my suffering." The wind was from the southeast, and the weather comparatively fair and pleasant. William Murphy found it to be impossible to get along, and he finally turned back during the day. Ultimately, Charles Burger was missed, and it was supposed that he had gone back. They struggled on until night, and encamped at the head of Truckee lake, about four miles from the mountain. The day following they resumed their painful and distressing journey; and after traveling all day, encamped on the west side of the main chain of the Sierra Nevada, about six miles from their last camp. They were without tents. The wind, on this and the previous day, was from the southeast. On the 18th they traveled five miles, and encamped. Mr. Stanton became snow-blind during the day, and fell back, but came up after they had been in camp an hour.

As several instances of snow-blindness will be mentioned in the subsequent progress of this narrative, I will here observe that it is produced by the glare of the snow, combined with great fatigue. It may be prevented, or its effects obviated, by the use of either dark green glasses or black handkerchiefs. Of these they had none.

December 19.—Although the wind was from the northwest, yet the snow which had fallen on the previous night, thawed a little. Mr. Stanton again fell behind, in consequence of blindness. He came up about an hour after they were encamped. The wind on the 20th was from the northeast. In the morning they resumed their journey, and guided by the sun, as they had hitherto been, they traveled until night. Mr. Stanton again fell behind. The wind next day changed to southwest, and the snow fell all day. They encamped at sunset, and about dark Mr. Stanton came up. They resumed their journey on the 22d, Mr. Stanton came into camp in about an hour, as usual. That night they consumed the last of their little stock of provisions. They had limited themselves to one ounce at each meal, since leaving the mountain camp, and now the last was gone. They had one gun, but they had not seen a living creature. The weather was clear and pleasant during the day, and the wind northeast. The weather was always clear when the wind was east or northeast. A south and southwest wind always brought a snow-storm.

December 23.—During this day Mr. Eddy examined a little bag for the purpose of throwing out something, with a view to getting along with more ease. In doing this, he found about half a pound of bear's meat, to which was attached a paper upon which his wife had written in pencil, a note signed "Your own dear Eleanor," in which she requested him to save it for the last extremity, and expressed the opinion that it would be the means of saving his life. This was really the case, for without it, he must subsequently have perished. On the morning of this day Mr. Stanton remained at the camp-fire, smoking his pipe. He requested them to go on, saying that he would overtake them. The snow was about fifteen feet deep. Mr. Stanton did not come up with them. On the morning of the 24th, they resumed their melancholy journey, and after traveling about a mile, they encamped to wait for their companion. They had nothing to eat during the day. Mr. Stanton did not come up. The snow fell all night, and increased one foot in depth. They now gave up poor Stanton for dead. A party that subsequently returned from the settlement, headed by Mr. Fallen, found his remains at the place where they had left him. His pistols, pipe, and some other articles, were found by him; but his body was in a great measure consumed by beasts of prey.

Mr. Stanton was from Syracuse, New York, and had been a merchant at that place. He was kind and benevolent in his feelings, and gentlemanly in his deportment and manners. He had, as has been stated in a previous part of this narrative, been sent on in company with Mr. McCutcheon from the Great Salt Lake, to obtain supplies from the settlements. He traveled several hundred miles through hostile Indians, across deserts and over lofty mountains. He arrived at Capt. Sutter's Fort about the first of October, and from this generous and noble man, obtained supplies for his suffering fellow-travelers. Furnished with seven mules loaded with provisions, and two Indian *vaqueros*, he returned, and met them at the crossing of Truckee river, about half way between Pyramid Lake and Truckee Lake — their route having led them within ten miles of the former. Had it not been for the disinterested sympathy of Mr. Stanton for the unfortunate emigrants, all must have perished before the first party sent out to their assistance reached them.

Before he left Capt. Sutter's Fort to return to their assistance, he left a vest in charge of that gentleman, in one of the pockets of which a small package was subsequently found, directed to Capt. Sutter, with a memorandum as follows: "Capt. Sutter will send the within, in the event of my death, to Sydney Stanton, Syracuse, N.Y." Inclosed was a diamond breast-pin, with a note from his sister, addressed to him at Chicago, Illinois, from which the following is an extract: "Sidney has requested me to do up your breast-pin, and send it to you. As you perceive, I have done it up in a newspaper. . . . . . May God bless you, my dear brother.

A. S."

The only entire article on the piece of newspaper, was the following translation for the True Sun, from the French: —

"THE WITHERED FLOWER.

"O! dying flower, that droop'st alone,
    Erewhile the valley's pride,
Thy withered leaves, disordered strown,
    Rude winds sweep far and wide.

"The scythe of Time, whose stroke we mourn,
    Our common doom shall bring.
From thee a faded leaf is torn,
    From us a joy takes wing.

"As life flies by, oh! who but feels
    Some sense, some charm decay?
E'en every fleeting moment steals
    Some treasured dream away.

"Some secret blight each hope destroys,
    Till at length we ask in grief,
If, than life's ephemeral joys,
    The floweret's be more brief."

Every one who understands a woman's heart, who has enjoyed a sister's love and confidence, and who observes the peculiar appropriateness of the poetry to the circumstances then surrounding this affectionate girl, will see in a moment that the paper was selected by her on that account.

On Christmas Day the painful journey was again continued, and after traveling two or three miles, the wind changed to the southwest. The snow beginning to fall, they all sat down to hold a council for the purpose of determining whether to proceed. All the men but Mr. Eddy refused to go forward. The women and Mr. Eddy declared they would go through or perish. Many reasons were urged for returning, and among others the fact that they had not tasted food for two days, and this after having been on an allowance of one ounce per meal. It was said that they must all perish for want of food. At length, Patrick Dolan proposed that they should cast lots to see who should die, to furnish food for those who survived. Mr. Eddy seconded the motion. William Foster opposed the measure. Mr. Eddy then proposed that two persons should take each a six-shooter, and fight until one or both were slain. This, too, was objected to. Mr. Eddy at length proposed that they should resume their journey, and travel on till some one died. This was finally agreed to, and they staggered on for about three miles, when they encamped. They had a small hatchet with them, and after a great deal of difficulty they succeeded in making a large fire. About 10 o'clock on Christmas night, a most dreadful storm of wind, snow, and hail, began to pour down upon their defenseless heads. While procuring wood for the fire, the hatchet, as if to add another drop of bitterness to a cup already overflowing, flew from the handle, and was lost in unfathomable snows. About 11 o'clock that memorable night, the storm increased to a perfect tornado, and in an instant blew away every spark of fire. Antoine perished a little before this from fatigue, frost, and hunger. The company, except Mr. Eddy and one or two others, were now engaged in alternatingly imploring God for mercy and relief. That night's bitter cries, anguish, and despair, never can be forgotten. Mr. Eddy besought his companions to get down upon blankets, and he would cover them up with other blankets; urging that the falling snow would soon cover them, and they could thus keep warm. In about two hours this was done. Before this, however, Mr. Graves was relieved by death from the horrors of that night. Mr. Eddy told him that he was dying. He replied that he did not care, and soon expired. They remained under the blankets all that night, until about 10 o'clock, A.M., of the 26th, when Patrick Dolan, becoming deranged, broke away from them, and getting out into the snow, it was with great difficulty that Mr. Eddy again got him under. They held him there by force until about 4 o'clock, P.M., when he quietly and silently sunk into the arms of death. He was from Dublin, Ireland. Lemuel Murphy became deranged on the night of the 26th, and talked much about food. On the morning of the 27th, Mr. Eddy blew up a powder-horn, in an effort to strike fire under the blankets. His face and hands were much burned. Mrs. McCutcheon and Mrs. Foster

28

were also burned, but not seriously. About 4 o'clock P.M., the storm died away, and the angry clouds passed off. Mr. Eddy immediately got out from under the blankets, and in a short time succeeded in getting fire into a large pine tree. His unhappy companions then got out; and having broken off boughs, they put them down, and lay upon them before the fire. The flame ascended to the top of the tree, and burned off great numbers of dead limbs, some of them as large as a man's body; but such was their weakness and indifference, that they did not seek to avoid them at all. Although the limbs fell thick, they did not strike.

On the morning of December 28th, they found themselves too weak to walk. The sensation of hunger was not so urgent, but it was evident to all that some substantial nourishment was necessary to recruit their bodies. The horrible expedient of eating human flesh was now again proposed. This Mr. Eddy declined doing, but his miserable companions cut the flesh from the arms and legs of Patrick Dolan, and roasted and ate it, averting their faces from each other, and weeping.

They gave some of this horrible food to Lemuel Murphy, with the hope that he would revive; but he continued to grow weaker, until at length the lamp of life, which had been flickering so long, went out, and the darkness of death covered him forever.

They were all reduced to mere skeletons. The skin upon the face, particularly, was drawn tight over the bones; the eyes were sunken, and had a fierce and wild expression. Perhaps the eye of a famishing tiger would have something of the same expression. But as death came on, the countenance became more settled and calm; the eyes retreated still farther back into the head, losing their fierceness; and the whole features assuming, in some cases, a sort of fixedness, while in others they exhibited a calm and gentle repose, illuminated by the expiring rays of departing reason; like the surface of a lake, no longer lashed by the tempest into foaming surges; but reflecting from its bosom the last rays of the setting sun, indicating that night will soon come on, and cover it with darkness. In other cases, however, some time after this, the expression of the countenance was horrid, ghastly, and restless. The eye was wild and fierce, up to the very moment when its fire was quenched in death forever.

To this place they gave the name of "The Camp of Death."* The horrors of that awful scene exceed the power of language to describe, or of imagination to conceive. Besides starvation, they had to contend also with trackless mountains and almost unfathomable snows. The wind and hail had beaten upon them with a fury that seemed to indicate that the Almighty had let loose the elements upon their devoted heads. The deep stupor into which their calamities had plunged the most of them, often changed to despair.

*Our book title takes editorial license with the specific usage here of this place name. — ed.

Each seemed to see inevitable destruction, and expressed in moans, sighs, and tears, the gloomy thoughts over which their minds were brooding. Mr. Eddy dissembled his own fears, and sought, by proferred consolations and an unmoved countenance, to inspire them with hope and courage. He found it impossible to dissipate the terror of the men. With his female companions there was less difficulty. Some of them, indeed, exhibited a want of fortitude; but the most of them manifested a constancy and courage, a coolness, presence of mind, and patience, which he had not, previous to entering upon this journey, suspected to form any part of female character. He had often occasion to remark the fortitude with which the most of the females sustained the sad reverses by which they were overwhelmed on the way. The difficulties, dangers, and misfortunes which frequently seemed to prostrate the men, called forth the energies of the gentler sex, and gave to them a sublime elevation of character, which enabled them to abide the most withering blasts of adversity with unshaken firmness. She who had been, while in prosperity, all weakness and dependence; clinging around her husband as the ivy does to the oak, now suddenly rose to be his comforter.

On the morning of December 29th they resumed their journey from "The Camp of Death." They had been guided heretofore, partly by the sun, and partly by the two Indian *vaqueros,* Lewis and Salvadore, but now Lewis, who spoke a little English, informed them that they were lost, and that he was, therefore, unable to guide them. They proceeded on, however, in the best way they could, until night, when they encamped. Mr. Eddy had now been a long time without food. The half-pound of roasted bear meat, which his "own dear Eleanor" had, by stealth, put into the bottom of his sack, had preserved his life up to this moment. And even now he felt no hunger—that almost intolerable and maddening sensation had long since passed away. His feelings were peculiar, but altogether indescribable. His companions told him that he was dying. He did not, however, believe them; and so informed them. But he felt that he was sinking, and that there was a rapid breaking up of his energies, which, under God, had hitherto saved his own life and that of his companions. Although he felt no hunger, his body imperiously demanded nourishment. Such were the circumstances under which he made his first cannibal meal. He experienced no loathing or disgust, but his reason, which he thought was never more unclouded, told him that it was a horrid repast. The hard hand of necessity was upon him, and he was compelled to eat or die.

This night passed away as tranquilly as could have been expected of persons situated as they were. Mr. Eddy talked with his unfortunate fellow-travelers of the means by which they would save themselves. He sought to reanimate them with courage, and to inspire them with hope, by speaking of their deliverance as certain. More than one vowed vengeance upon Hastings, for having decoyed them into his cut-off. Their feelings will perhaps be understood by those whom Jesse Applegate, in a similar manner, decoyed into the "Applegate cut-off."

On the morning of December 30th they resumed their journey, their feet being so swollen that they had burst open, and, although they were wrapped in rags and pieces of blankets, yet it was with great pain and difficulty that they made any progress. They encamped, late in the afternoon, upon the high bank of a very deep cañon. From this point they could distinctly see a valley which they believed to be the valley of the Sacramento.

December 31st was spent in crossing the cañon, and although they toiled hard during the entire day, they effected no more than the crossing. Every foot of that day's struggle was marked with the blood from their feet. They encamped that night on the banks of the cañon. Here Mr. Eddy saw that poor Jay Fosdick would not survive much longer; and reminded him that his end was nigh, if he did not summon up all his energies.

On this night they ate the last flesh of their deceased companions. One of the company then proposed that they should kill the two Indian boys, Lewis and Salvadore, who, it will be remembered, met them with Mr. Stanton, with provisions for their relief; Mr. Eddy remonstrated, but finding that the deed was resolved upon, he determined to prevent it by whatever means God and nature might enable him to use. Desiring, however, to avoid extremities, if possible, he secretly informed Lewis of the fate that awaited him and his companion, and concluded by advising him to fly. The expression of the face of Lewis, never can be forgotten; he did not utter one word in reply, but stood in mute astonishment. In about two minutes his features settled into Indian sullenness, and he turned away to fly from the scene of danger. Their complicated sufferings were of a character that rendered it impossible for them to judge accurately, of the right or wrong of many actions. But this was a deed which nothing could justify or excuse. Had it been proposed to cast lots for the purpose of determining who should die, and the lot had fallen upon these Indians, or upon Mr. Eddy, he would have submitted to it without a murmur or complaint. But the thing proposed, he could not but regard with feelings of abhorrence. His very soul recoiled at the thought.

January 1, 1847.—They made their New Year's dinner of the strings of their snow-shoes. Mr. Eddy also ate an old pair of moccasins. They struggled on until night, and encamped in six feet snow. On the morning of the following day they resumed their journey, their feet being still greatly swollen and cracked, and encamped at night in three feet snow. That night they took some old boots and shoes, and having slightly crisped them in the fire, made an evening meal of them.

They staggered on during the 3d, and encamped at night on bare ground, the snow, however, being still in patches. The whole face of the country had gradually changed; the hills had become less and less rugged, and they were now encamped in an open oak grove. They had nothing to eat during this long and melancholy night. Mr. Eddy saw that death was beginning to grapple with poor Jay Fosdick. He had been sinking for some time; but now it was evident that he was drawing very near to the close of his sorrowful pilgrimage. He also saw that they would all very soon perish, if they did not obtain relief. He therefore determined secretly to leave the camp, and go on with a gun, hoping, now they had left the snows behind, that he would find some game. If successful, it was his purpose to return and share with his companions. If successful, he might save himself and them; if otherwise, he could but die. Finally, he determined to give the company some hint of his plans. They at once comprehended his purpose, and the women besought him not to leave them; assuring him that their only hope for life, was in his continuing with them.

On the morning of the 4th, Mary Graves, who had more strength than any of the other women, resolved that she would go with him or perish. Mrs. Pike threw her arms around his neck, imploring him, by every thing to which she could appeal, not to leave them. The other women added their tears and entreaties to those of Mrs. Pike. But to remain with them was to die. To go forward might possibly be the means of their preservation. Although they had seen no game nor a living thing since they had left the Mountain Camp, they were now in an open country, and this circumstance, although trifling in itself, was one that afforded him a hope. Those who have not been in situations in which they were exposed to extreme peril, can form no correct conception of the value which sometimes attaches to the simplest object. They can never know with what desperate eagerness and energy one seizes upon the slightest means capable of mitigating the rigor of a fate into which their circumstances seem about to plunge them.

Mary Graves and Mr. Eddy accordingly set forward. They had not proceeded above two miles, when they came to where a deer had lain the previous night. In an instant a feeling took possession of his heart to which it had been a stranger. He knew not what were all the elements of his emotions; but gratitude to God, and a hope in his providence were at least two. Tears immediately began to flow down his haggard cheeks. He turned round and saw Mary weeping like a child. As soon as his choked utterance would admit of his speaking, he said, "Mary, don't you feel like praying?" "Oh, yes," she replied with sobs and tears, "I do, but I never prayed in my life! Do you pray?" He replied that he knew not how to pray. But in an instant they were both upon their knees, and by a feeling natural to the unfortunate, their hearts were turned toward heaven. Surrounded by danger, and not having a prayer-book, they addressed themselves to the invisible Being in terms neither studied nor measured, but which were the spontaneous outburstings of hearts that felt that nothing but the God who maintains the order of the universe could afford them succor in this their last and most fearful extremity. They then rose from their knees, experiencing the cheering influence of hope. Their vows were solemn and their prayers fervent and impassioned. There was in that first prayer a luxury, the remembrance of which was delightful. In all Mr. Eddy's anguish of spirit upon this most disastrous road he had not shed a tear. Some had wept and prayed; others had wept and cursed Almighty God for their hard fate. He had never felt like cursing God, or blaming his Providence; but he had not wept. The fountains of his tears were as dry as many of the deserts over which they had passed, and upon which they had wrecked their little fortunes. Tears would have relieved the agony of a spirit which, although not disposing him to blaspheme his Maker, did not incline him to submit to the chastisement of his hand. But now he had wept and prayed, and rose from his knees, feeling an humble but not presumptuous trust, that God would fill his mouth with food, and his heart with gladness. They had not proceeded far before they saw a large buck, about eighty yards distant. Mr. Eddy raised his rifle, and for some time tried to bring it to bear upon the deer; but such was his extreme weakness that he could not. He breathed a little, changing his manner of holding the gun, and made another effort. Again his weakness prevented him from being able to hold upon it. He heard a low and suppressed sobbing behind him, and turning round saw Mary Graves weeping and in great agitation, her head bowed, and her hands upon her face. Alarmed lest she should cause the deer to run, Mr. Eddy begged her to be quiet, which she did, after exclaiming, "O, I am afraid you will not kill it!" He brought the gun up to his face the third time, and elevating the muzzle above the deer, let it descend, until he saw the animal through the sights, when the rifle cracked. The deer bounded up about three feet, and then stood still. Mary immediately wept aloud, exclaiming, "O, merciful God, you have missed it!" Mr. Eddy assured her that he had not; that he knew the rifle was upon it the moment of firing; and that, in addition to this, the deer had dropped its tail between its legs, which this animal always does when wounded. They were at the moment standing upon a precipice of about thirty feet, a snow-bank being at the bottom. In a short time the deer ran. Mr. Eddy immediately sprang down the precipice, and in a moment Mary followed him. The deer ran about two hundred yards, and fell. Mr. Eddy got to it while it was yet alive, and taking it by the horns, cut its throat with a pen-knife. Before this was done, Mary was at his side, and they drank the blood together as it flowed from the expiring beast. This gave to them a little strength, and with their faces all covered with blood, they sat down to rest a little. In a short time they rolled the deer near by to a spot where they made a fire. That night they ate the entrails; and with their hearts glowing with gratitude to the Giver of all good, they enjoyed a degree of refreshing slumber to which they had long been strangers.

Their dreams were wont to tantalize and mock them with rich and varied food, prepared in the most inviting manner. But this night they had made an abundant meal upon the entrails of the deer—a meal that they enjoyed more than any they had ever eaten; and their rest was not broken by dreams that insulted their misfortunes.

They rose on the morning of the 5th of January, filled with renewed hopes, and deeply impressed with the sublime idea of a Great and Good Being extending a protecting aegis over the unfortunate.

Several times during the night of the 4th, Mr. Eddy had fired his rifle for the purpose of informing his companions where they were. Jay Fosdick, who, it will be remembered, was expected to die, was about a mile back. He had lain down, unable to proceed any further; and his wife was with him. Upon hearing Mr. Eddy's rifle crack, at the time of his killing the deer, he exclaimed, in a feeble voice—"There! Eddy has killed a deer. Now, if I can only get to him, I shall live." William Foster and wife, Mrs. Pike, and Mrs. McCutcheon, were encamped about half way between Mr. Eddy's camp, and the place at which Mr. Fosdick and his wife were. One of the emigrants, believing that Mr. and Mrs. Fosdick had died during the previous night, sent a person back to the place, with instructions to get Mrs. Fosdick's heart for breakfast; and to be sure to secure her jewelry, and her husband's watches and money. The person sent for this purpose met Mrs. Fosdick on the way to Mr. Eddy's camp. The individual thus sent turned about, and came on with her to Mr. Eddy's camp; who gave them some of the roasted liver of the deer, and upon their returning to the other camp, he requested that all should come to him, and partake of his venison.

Mrs. Fosdick had been with her husband during the previous night, which was bitterly cold; and after his death, she rolled his body in the only blanket they possessed, and laid herself down upon the ground, desiring to die, and hoping that she would freeze to death. The scenes surrounding her were rendered still more terrible by the horror inspired by the darkness of the night; and she prayed, and in a certain sense, struggled for death, during the whole of its heavily-passing hours. But the return of the morning's light brought with it an instinctive love of life, and she now proposed to go back to the body of her husband, and for the last time kiss his lips, then cold and silent in death. Two individuals accompanied her, and when they arrived at the body, they, notwithstanding the remonstrances, entreaties, and tears of the afflicted widow, cut out the heart and liver, and severed the arms and legs of her departed husband.

Mrs. Fosdick took up a little bundle she had left, and returned with these two persons to one of the camps, where she saw an emigrant thrust the heart through with a stick, and hold it in the fire to roast. Unable to endure the horrible sight of seeing literally devoured a heart that had fondly and ardently loved her until it had ceased to throb, she turned away, and went to another camp, sick and almost blinded by the spectacle.

Mr. Eddy cut up the deer, dried it before his fire, and then divided it with his unhappy companions in misfortune and peril, of both camps.

The day having thus passed away, on the morning of the 6th of January they all started together. They went down to the north branch of the American fork of the Sacramento, and after crossing it, encamped for the night. They resumed their journey the next morning, and being unable to proceed down the river, they commenced climbing a very high and difficult mountain. The sides were very steep, and they pulled themselves up the rocks, by laying hold of shrubs growing in crevices. There were many places in which, had these given way, they would have been precipitated hundreds of feet below.

Their feet were greatly bruised, and so swollen that they had literally burst open, and were bleeding so much, that the fragments of blankets with which they were bound up, were saturated with blood. But a merciful God assisted them in a wonderful manner; and after struggling all day, they reached the top, where they encamped. The day was fine, and although the minds of the company were singularly altered by untold sufferings, yet the most perfect tranquillity reigned among them, as calms are said sometimes to precede the most desolating storms. Mr. Eddy lamented the loss of their unfortunate companions, but carefully avoided making any allusion to recent revolting events. They sat down upon the ground to their evening repast, and consumed the last of their venison.

Soon after, Eddy and Foster were apart from the company. Despondency had again seized upon the mind of the latter. He had all along exhibited evidences of a partial and, perhaps, perfect insanity, caused by mental anxiety, hardships, and perils. He had also shown, as a consequence of this, a total want of energy, making no effort, rendering no assistance in making fires, and seeming to look to Mr. Eddy, and to depend upon him—as, indeed, did all the company—to guide and save the lives of the party. He doubted not that they were approaching the last critical hour of their fate. Suffering and danger had rendered him selfish to the last degree; and seeming firmly to believe that the sacrifice of the lives of some of their companions was necessary to the preservation of the others, he proposed to kill Mrs. McCutcheon, alleging that she was but a nuisance, and could not keep up. Mr. Eddy remonstrated, and told him that she was a wife and a mother, and was with them, helpless and without protection, unless she found it in them; and finally informed him, with much sternness in his manner, that she should not die. Foster then proposed that they should kill Mary Graves and Mrs. Fosdick, as they had no children. Mr. Eddy told him that he would inform them of his purpose. This he did in the presence of the company. Foster said he did not care, he could handle Mr. Eddy. Seeing that he was lost to all reason, and perfectly insane, and firmly believing that they would all fall a sacrifice to his insane appetite, unless the further development of this spirit of selfishness was checked, Mr. Eddy said, "Perhaps you intend to make a victim of me. If this is so, we will proceed to settle the question." Seizing a large club, and striking it across a log, to ascertain whether it would break, Mr. Eddy threw it to him, and bade him defend himself. At the same time he advanced upon him with a knife which had belonged to Jay Fosdick, as rapidly as he could in his weak and feeble condition, with the intention of taking his life. Having gotten almost within striking distance, with his arm raised to strike a fatal blow, he was seized by Mary Graves, Mrs. Pike, Mrs. McCutcheon, and Mrs. Fosdick, and thrown down. The knife was then taken away from him. He then told Foster, who stood apparently powerless, that he would kill him if he ever again manifested the slightest inclination to take the life of any of the party; and that if it should become necessary to take life, in order to the preservation of other lives, one of them should be the victim; and that this point should be determined by fighting, since Foster had shown a determination not to cast lots, which was the only just method of deciding upon the victim. Foster might easily, had he possessed the energy, have dispatched Eddy at the time when the females, whose lives he had saved, by resolutely resisting Mr. Foster's purpose, had thrown him down. But devoid of energy, and conscious, perhaps, although he could not have been sane, that he had meditated a wicked act, he cowered before Eddy's look.

On the other hand, Mr. Eddy was conscious of doing right; and, in addition to this, his was a courage animated by desperation. He had left behind him in the Sierra Nevada a most beloved and affectionate wife, and two young children, whom he tenderly loved. He had been unable to take them out, and was now staggering into the settlements for the purpose of obtaining the means of rescuing them. He saw that Foster was evidently deranged, and therefore a dangerous man to be with, in the circumstances in which they were then placed; and while he was willing to share the risk of life incident to their situation, yet, the ghastly images of his famine-stricken wife and children appealed to every generous feeling of his nature, to require of others a similar and equal risk. He might have reached the settlements sooner, perhaps, by consenting to the death of his companions; but had he done this, and thereby have saved his wife and children, the remembrance of the price paid would have embittered every subsequent moment of his miserable being.

The morning of Jan. 8th they resumed their journey from the "Camp of Strife," order being re-established. They had not proceeded above two miles, when they came into a small patch of snow, where they found the tracks of Lewis and Salvadore, for the first time since Mr. Eddy informed them of their danger. Foster immediately said that he would follow them, and kill them if he came up with them. They had not proceeded more than two miles when they came upon the Indians, lying upon the ground, in a totally helpless condition. They had been without food for eight or nine days, and had been four days without fire. They could not, probably, have lived more than two or three hours; nevertheless, Eddy remonstrated against their being killed. Foster affirmed that he was compelled to do it. Eddy refused to see the deed consummated, and went on about two hundred yards, and halted. Lewis was told that he must die; and was shot through the head. Salvadore was dispatched in the same manner immediately after. Mr. Eddy did not see who fired the gun. The flesh was then cut from their bones and dried. Mr. Foster and wife, and Mrs. Pike encamped at "The Place of Sacrifice." Mary Graves, Mrs. Fosdick, Mrs. McCutcheon, and Mr. Eddy encamped about two hundred yards in advance. They never encamped again with Foster; and some one of their number was always awake, to avoid being surprised.

Mr. Eddy made his supper upon grass. Although they saw deer in great numbers every day, and sometimes very near them, yet such was the extreme weakness to which Mr. Eddy was reduced, that it was impossible for him to take accurate aim at them. He staggered like a drunken man; and when he came to a fallen tree, though no more than a foot high, he had to stoop down, put his

MEETING WITH THE INDIANS.

hands upon it, and get over it by a sort of rolling motion. They were under the necessity of sitting down to rest about every quarter of a mile. The slightest thing caused them to stumble and fall. They were almost reduced to the helplessness of little children in their first essays to walk. The women would fall and weep like infants, and then rise and totter along again.

January 9.—They proceeded during the day over a rocky country, and encamped at night, after a day of immense toil and suffering. Mr. Eddy gathered some grass near by, to sustain, in his wasted body, the almost extinguished spark of life.

On the following morning they staggered forward, and toward the close of the day, which seemed interminable, they arrived at an Indian village, which in this country is called a *rancheria*. The Indians seemed to be overwhelmed with the sight of their miseries.

Proverbial as they are for their cruelty and thievish propensities, they now divided their own scanty supply with them. The wild and fierce savages who once visited their camps only for the purpose of hostility; who hovered around them upon the way; who shot their cattle, and murdered their companions; who actually stood upon the hills, laughing at their calamity, and mocking as their fear came, now seemed touched with the sight of their misfortunes; and their almost instinctive feeling of hostility to the white man, gave place to pity and commiseration. The men looked as solemn as the grave; the women wrung their hands and wept aloud; the children united their plaintive cries to those of their sympathizing mothers. As soon as the first brief burst of feeling had subsided, all united in administering to their wants. One hurried here, and another there, all sobbing and weeping, to obtain their stores of acorns. The acorns grow upon a species of the live oak, and are from one to two inches in length. They are in appearance and taste very much like the chestnut. While they were eating these the Indian women began to prepare a sort of bread from the acorns, pulverized. As fast as they could bake them, they gave them to starving emigrants. It was a sort of food that made Mr. Eddy sick, producing constipation. It did not affect the others in this manner.

On the morning of January 11th, the chief, after sending on runners to the next village, informing them of the approach of the sufferers and to prepare food for them, accompanied them during the day with many of his tribe, an Indian being on either side of each of the sufferers, supporting them, and assisting them forward. They thus continued from day to day until the morning of the 17th, the chief from one village accompanied by some of his men, supporting them to the next, where they witnessed the same exhibition of feeling and sympathy. They received the best food the Indians had, which was acorns. But this, as I before remarked, made Mr. Eddy sick, and he could not eat them, but had lived upon grass only. On the morning of this day, the chief, with much difficulty and labor, procured for him about a gill of pine-nuts, which he ate, and found himself wonderfully refreshed.

They resumed their journey on the next morning, as usual, accompanied by a chief and a number of Indians, supporting and assisting them. Mr. Eddy felt a renewed strength, derived in part, as he supposed, from the pine-nuts, and in part, from the energy which a prospect of a speedy termination of his unhappy journey imparted. Nature seemed to have gathered up all her strength for the last effort; so that he was even able to proceed without assistance.

They had not gone more than a mile when the whole party, excepting Mr. Eddy, sunk under their complicated toils and sufferings, and all laid down to die. The Indians appeared to be greatly distressed. But the picture of his wife and children, perishing with hunger among the terrible snows of the Sierra Nevada, filled the spirit of Mr. Eddy with unspeakable anguish, and he resolved to get to where relief for them could be obtained, or to perish by the way. The old chief sent an Indian with him, instructing him, as well as Mr. E. could understand, to take him to the nearest settlement.

Mr. Eddy had suffered unutterable sorrows by the way. Fear and anguish had got hold upon him; and although he believed that his reason was never more unclouded, yet continued anxiety, the most cruel privations, and circumstances presenting the severest tests of principle, had changed his feelings and his nature in a considerable degree. Let it not therefore be imagined, that in all the dangers surrounding him he had preserved himself entire, if I may be permitted thus to express myself. Now he felt that he was escaping from a painful dream of combats, of famine and death; of cries of despair; of fathomless snows, and impassable mountains; dreams that tormented his soul and exhausted his body with fatigue. The scene was changed. The day was calm and beautiful, and the sun shone as bright as though no murder had ever been committed in its light. A ray of hope beamed to quiet his agitated and over-wrought spirit. He expected soon to be once more among the abodes of society and civilization, and to be able to send succor to his wife and children.

Thus situated, and thus feeling, he hastened on, as though famine and death were close upon the heels of himself and his family. They had not proceeded more than five miles, when they met another Indian, to whom Mr. Eddy promised some tobacco, if he would accompany them. At last it became necessary for them to assist him; and they hurried forward until they arrived at the house of Col. M. D. Richey, about half an hour before sunset, having traveled eighteen miles. The last six miles of the way were marked by the blood from Mr. Eddy's feet. The first white woman he saw, was the daughter of the truly excellent Mr. Richey. Mr. Eddy asked her for bread. She looked at him, and without replying, burst into tears, and took hold of him to assist him into the house. He was immediately placed in bed, in which, during four days, he was not able to turn his body. In a very short time he had food brought to him by Mrs. Richey, who sobbed as she fed the miserable and frightful being before her. In a brief period Harriet, the daughter, had carried the news from house to house in the little neighborhood; and horses were seen running at full speed from place to place, until all the necessary preparations were made for taking out relief to those Mr. Eddy had left in the morning. William Johnson, John Howell, John Rhodes, Mr. Kiser, Mr. Segur, Daniel Tucker, and Joseph Varro, assembled at Mr. Richey's immediately. The females collected all the bread they had, with tea, sugar, and coffee; amounting in the whole to as much as four men could conveniently carry. Howell, Rhodes, Segur, and Tucker, immediately started on foot, with the Indians for guides, and arrived at the company, eighteen miles distant, about midnight. One man was employed all night in cooking food, and although Mr. Eddy had cautioned these gentlemen not to give the sufferers as much as they desired, yet the provisions were all consumed that night. They wept and begged for food continually, until it was exhausted. It is needless to say that they were all sick; none, however, died.

On the morning of Jan. 18th, Mr. Richey, William Johnson, Joseph Varro, and Mr. Kiser, proceeded on horseback, with more provisions for the emigrants, and to bring them in. About 10 o'clock at night they returned, surprised at the distance Mr. Eddy had traveled, which they said they could not have believed, had they not passed over it. Mr. Richey remarked when he returned, that he had followed Mr. Eddy's track six miles by the blood from his feet.

The 19th was a beautiful day, and although Mr. Eddy felt great solicitude for his family, his soul was in harmony with the aspect of the heavens, which seemed to shed upon him a new ray of hope. Filled with gratitude for his own deliverance, he sought to obtain immediate relief for those who yet remained in the Sierra Nevada. For this purpose he dictated a letter to John Sinclair, Alcalde of the Upper District, residing near Sutter's Fort, about forty miles distant, informing him of the condition and peril of the emigrants, and urging him to adopt measures for their immediate rescue from famine, cannibalism, and death. An Indian courier was sent with it. Mrs. Sinclair sent back by the Indian a considerable amount of under-clothing for the females of Mr. Eddy's party, who had arrived almost in a state of nudity.

Mr. Sinclair immediately dispatched a courier to San Francisco with a letter containing the intelligence. The letter was taken up to the City Hotel, and read at the tea-table. The scene that followed will never be forgotten by those present. The ladies immediately left the table, sobbing and in tears. The men, overwhemed with the picture of distress it presented, rose in haste; and many an eye unused to tears, expressed how much was felt by the burthened and sickened heart.

Preparations for Relieving the Sufferers

THE insurrection, which had entirely occupied the attention of the United States officers, and of all classes of citizens in the northern district of California, of which San Francisco was the "headquarters"—having been entirely suppressed, and order restored by the middle of January, 1847, Mr. Reed, who, in consequence of that insurrection, had not been able to obtain any assistance which would aid him in making another effort to recross the mountains, now hoped to effect something, at the earliest moment that experienced mountaineers, acquainted with the Sierra Nevada, believed that sufficient intervals would elapse between the storms in that elevated region, and the settling of the snows, to warrant such an undertaking. Experienced men supposed this might occur by the last of February or first of March; although such an attempt must ever be attended with much risk and no little suffering to the party who should undertake it before the melting of the snows.

At this time Mr. Reed was at the Pueblo de San Jose, on the southeast side of San Francisco Bay, about one hundred and twenty miles from Sutter's Fort. His situation, and that of his suffering companions in misfortune, soon became known to the whole people. Among the people in the town and immediate vicinity, particularly the Mission of Santa Clara, were many immigrants of the last season, who had got in safely and in good time by the old Fort Hall road; and also some who had been caught on and near the summit of the Sierra, in the month of December, 1844, but had got through the snows themselves with great difficulty, leaving behind them all their property, most of which was destroyed by the Indians, in the spring of 1845, before they could recross the mountains to recover it.

Great sympathy was expressed for Mr. Reed and the sufferers, by all parties, as they feared that the company must soon be in a starving condition. Nothing, however, was done.

Mr. Reed, perceiving that nothing could be done at San Jose, proceeded to San Francisco, to bring the condition of the sufferers to the knowledge of the Governor, by a personal representation;

and with that view called upon the Alcalde of the town and district of San Francisco, Washington A. Bartlett, Lieutenant U. S. Navy, who at once took a lively interest in all his statements, and assured him that assistance should certainly be afforded him, and that immediately. Lieut. Bartlett waited upon the Governor, and introduced Mr. Reed, who told his painful story; when Capt. Hull stated that he had that morning received a petition from the Pueblo de San Jose; but as he had neither the men nor means to fit out such an expedition as the petition called for, he would consult with the Alcalde, and see what could be done. He remarked, that he thought petitions would do but little toward affording relief, if that was all the people were disposed to do. Lieut. Bartlett informed him that, from what he had already learned in conversation with the principal citizens of the town, a very liberal subscription could be obtained, and a relief company started in a very short time, if the Governor would give it his countenance and support. Governor Hull stated that he would do all in his power, both officially and as a private citizen, and that relief must be sent.

Lieut. Bartlett then informed the Governor that he would issue a call for a public meeting that evening, when the Governor authorized him to subscribe fifty dollars on his account. Capt. Mervine, U. S. Navy, and Mr. Richardson, U. S. Collector, subscribed the same amount.

The meeting was at once called; and at 7, P.M., February 3d, nearly every male citizen of San Francisco, and the officers of the United States forces, assembled in the saloon of the principal hotel, to consider what should be done.

His Honor the Alcalde called the meeting to order, by reading his call upon them to assemble; and then, after stating that Governor Hull designed to do all he could in the matter, read to the meeting the petition from San Jose, and expressed his belief that, although the citizens of San Francisco had never before been called upon to exercise a collective charity, this call would result in something more than petition; but that, as he did not wish to forestall their action by his suggestions, he hoped they would organize the meeting independently of the magistracy, and thus afford him an opportunity of acting in his private capacity with his fellow-citizens and brother officers. Frank Ward, Esq., was then called to the chair, and William Pettet, Esq., was appointed secretary.

Mr. Reed having come into the room, the people desired him to state to them his opinion of what would be required to make an expedition successful in its results. But Mr. Reed begged to decline, alleging that his feelings were such, that he could not command himself sufficiently to express himself publicly, with the conviction ever on his mind that, in all probability, his wife and children were then starving. Overpowered with emotion by the delivery of a few remarks, he sat down with tears streaming from his eyes, and showing how severe was his suffering.

Mr. Dunleary, with whom Mr. Reed lodged (himself an immigrant), now rose, and stated that, in conversation with Mr. Reed at his house, he had gathered his views, and that he himself had traveled the road, and supposed he could estimate pretty closely where the company then must be; he would, with the indulgence of the meeting, give the views of Mr. Reed and himself as to what was best to be done.

Those who heard that thrilling address of Mr. Dunleary will never forget the effect upon his attentive audience, while he related the trials of their journey and the probable fate of the starving company, unless relief was soon carried to them—perhaps already too late; but it was hoped that, if prudent, they could hold out till the first of March. (It must be remembered that nearly the entire population of San Francisco, then resident there, were immigrants by sea, and entirely unacquainted with life on the road or in the mountains.) It is worthy of notice, that the sufferers encamped on the very spot (Truckee Lake) where Mr. Dunleary supposed they must have arrived the day the first snow fell, which was only thirty miles beyond the point reached by Reed and McCutcheon when they failed in their first effort.

The speaker had scarcely taken his seat, when the people rushed up to the chairman's table, from all parts of the hall, with their hands full of dollars. But the chairman begged they would stay their hands for a moment, and organize a little; when two committees were elected—one to solicit subscriptions (scarcely necessary), and also a treasurer, and a committee of purchases of supplies. These were instructed to consult with the Alcalde, who was requested to act with both committees. The subscription was then opened, and $700 subscribed before the meeting adjourned.

Messrs. Ward and Smith, in addition to a generous subscription, offered their fine launch, *"Dice mi Nana,"* free of charge, to transport the expedition to Feather river. Mr. John Fuller volunteered to pilot the launch, and Passed-midshipman Woodworth, U. S. N., volunteered to take charge of the expedition, under instructions from the committee and Governor, and carry out the wishes of the people in aiding Mr. Reed to save the sufferers.

The committee at once dispatched a courier to the Redwood, forty miles south, for Mr. Dennis Martin, as it was not known that any other person could be had who could pilot in the mountains, when covered with snow. A pilot was all-important to prevent the loss of the party going out—at least to take the very shortest route to Truckee's lake.

The next day was employed in adding to the subscription, and purchasing any thing in the market which the best judgment could suggest as necessary. Howard Oakley volunteered to go with Mr. Woodworth, and men were obtained to work the launch up the river. The utmost expedition was used to get Messrs. Woodworth and Reed started. The courier returned from the Redwood, stating that Mr. Martin could not possibly go, in consequence of his engagements.

On the 5th all was ready for a start with the evening tide, when Captain Sutter's launch, "Sacramento," appeared off the town, and on anchoring, the Alcalde received from Justice Sinclair a letter, which, while it filled the hearts of all with horror by its terrible details; and incited to additional efforts of relief, was softened by the pleasing reflection that they had not waited for such an appeal to move them to action.

That letter, honorable to the writer and Captain Sutter, and well calculated to rouse to exertion, was at once laid before Governor Hull, and read at the tables of the principal hotels, by the committees and citizens generally; and, as it contained the information so much needed, enabled the committees of relief to act more understandingly. It being now known that a relief-party were actually on the route, and would probably succeed in bringing out of the snows a considerable number of the sufferers, it was determined to make every provision necessary to relieve both the sufferers and those who had gone to their aid, and to have a relief-camp established at the most eligible point on the route, and also to provide liberally for the wants of the emigrants, in food and clothing, should any party succeed in getting them out. It was, therefore, determined to increase the funds during the next day, and thus increase the supplies, in all that could be considered useful.

The same evening, February 5th, Mr. Greenwood, an old mountaineer, also appeared at San Francisco to ask for assistance in fitting out a party to go out with himself and McCutcheon, to which end the citizens of Sonoma and Nappa, headed by Lieutenant William L. Maury, U. S. N., Commandant of the port, and Don Mariaño G. Vallejo, Ex-Commandant-general of California, had subscribed over $500 for the party, besides large donations of horses and mules, which $500 was to be paid Greenwood and company, *if they succeeded* in raising a party and going out; but as warm clothing and ready money were absolutely necessary to start an expedition, they went to San Francisco for them. Greenwood thought he would succeed, if he could secure ten or twelve men he could depend upon in the snow. He believed he could secure such men by having ready money. His horses and provisions were already in his camp, at the head of Nappa valley.

Governor Hull now desired Lieutenant Bartlett to lay before him a statement of what was proposed to be done, as a basis for his action, on the part of the government; trusting to its generosity and humanity in sustaining him in an extraordinary expense which his position as Governor and Military Commandant of the Northern Department called upon him not to hesitate in incurring, even at the risk of its not being allowed by the government; and, on receiving from Lieutenant Bartlett a communication setting forth the facts already stated, and the appeal of Greenwood for aid to start his expedition, Captain Hull determined to appropriate $400 on government account to organize that party. Greenwood stated to Captain Hull, that he could easily get men, if he had this ready money to make advances and purchase clothing; and, as he had crossed the Sierra Nevada, while the snow lay on the summit, in April, 1846, he thought he could do it again, as soon as he could reach the mountain; and, possibly, he might succeed in driving over some of his horses, which he would kill in the Mountain Camp for provision for the sufferers. At any rate he and his sons, with Turner and others, could reach them on snow shoes.

As it was believed that Mr. Reed could get to the mountains quicker, by going via Sonoma and Nappa valleys, he determined to leave the next day with Mr. Greenwood, and get animals and packs prepared to meet Mr. Woodworth, at Feather river. Fifty dollars in money was given to Mr. Reed, by the committee, to pay contingencies, and an order, signed by Capt. Hull, to enable him to get the horses, and secure some men if possible. Greenwood was also to start on his independent expedition, at the earliest possible moment. Messrs. Reed and McCutcheon were supplied gratis by the committee, with every thing they required for the journey; and to Mr. Reed was also given a supply of clothing and goods, necessary for the women, who had already reached Johnson's. Mr. Reed was further directed, that in case he should have to waste any time at Feather river, for Mr. Woodworth's arrival, he was not to do so, but push on, and, if possible, drive some cattle to the edge of the snow, to relieve the party now known to be out; in which case, Mr. Woodworth had orders to get his horses, packs, and men, from Sutter's Fort; and if he could not take all on at once, Capt. Sutter was charged with the forwarding of the supplies, which he should leave behind. And Mr. Woodworth was to unload the launch at the Fort, if he should think he could get on faster by so doing.

During the 6th, the crews of the U. S. frigate Savannah, sloop of war Warren, and the marines, in garrison, on shore, carried the subscription up to $1300, which enabled the committee to get other necessaries; and, besides, to place in Mr. Woodworth's hands $100, with which to purchase cattle to drive as far as the snow, and then kill them for food for the relief-parties and sufferers. Capt. Hull, also, sent orders to Capts. Kern and Sutter, to do all in their power, by assisting with men and horses, to hurry forward the supplies.

On an application to Capt. Mervine, commanding the U. S. frigate Savannah, by Lieut. Bartlett, on the part of the committee of supplies, he furnished from the provisions of the ship twenty days' full rations for ten men or two hundred rations; that there should not be any expenditure of the supplies by the persons who should work the launch up and back.

Mr. Greenwood, with the $400 supplied to him by Capt. Hull, purchased the clothing necessary for his party, retaining the balance to make advances, and purchase provisions. All parties being thus supplied, so far as their necessities could be foreseen, set out on their errands of mercy. Messrs. Mellus and Howard tendered the gratuitous use of their launch to transport Messrs. Reed, Greenwood, McCutcheon, and others, to Sonoma.

GEORGIA A. DONNER.
(MRS. W. A. BABCOCK.)
1879.

ELIZA P. DONNER.
(MRS. S. O. HOUGHTON.)

W. C. GRAVES.
1879.

MARY A. GRAVES.
(MRS. J. T. CLARK.)
1879.

Mr. Glover's Two Expeditions
for the Relief of the Sufferers

It will be seen from the foregoing chapter, that an expedition was fitted out at San Francisco, for the relief of the emigrants at the Mountain Camp. But as another was organized a little before that, I will take it up as being the first in point of time.

In about a week after Mr. Sinclair received the letter, which has been mentioned as having been dictated by Mr. Eddy, he came to the place at which Mr. Eddy was temporarily abiding. Capt. E. Kern had made an unsuccessful effort to induce men to go with relief to the immigrants, offering three dollars per day. Aquilla Glover, R. S. Mootrey, and Joseph Sel, were all that would consent to go; and they were willing to enter upon the hazardous enterprise, without any other reward than the satisfaction derived from a consciousness of the fact that they might be instrumental, in the hands of God, in rescuing from the jaws of a miserable death a multitude of men, women, and children.

John Sinclair, Esq., and Mr. George McKinstry, Jr., returned from San Francisco about the time of the failure of the effort made by Capt. Kern. Capt. Sutter and Mr. Sinclair then proposed, that they would become responsible for three dollars per day, which they would pay, if the Government of the United States would not. This induced Daniel Rhodes, John Rhodes, Daniel Tucker, and Edward Coffeymier, to join the three above mentioned. William Koon, and a man for whom I have never known any other name than that of "Greasy Jim," also joined the expedition; but as these did not go through, no other notice will be taken of them. Capt. Sutter and John Sinclair furnished supplies and horses.

On the last day of January, the party set out, and after traveling fourteen miles, encamped on Dry Creek.

February 1.—Immediately after sunrise, Mr. Glover, who had command of the party, set out, and after traveling all day, encamped about three miles below Mr. Johnson's, on Bear river. The party proceeded, the next day, on to Mr. Johnson's, where the company was occupied during the 3d and 4th, in making pack-saddles, drying beef, and in completing the preparations for the journey. Mr. Eddy had greatly improved in strength, and fancying that he could be serviceable, he here determined to accompany the expedition.

On the 5th, the party set forward; and after being helped upon a horse, Mr. Eddy proceeded on with it. They continued traveling, with some delays, till February 9, when they arrived at the Mule Springs. Here they found the snow so deep that it became necessary to leave the horses. And such was Mr. Eddy's weak and feeble condition, that the party refused to permit him to go any further. The 10th was occupied in making preparations for carrying provisions over on foot.

The following day Mr. Eddy started back for the settlements, intending to procure fresh supplies, and to return with two men to meet Mr. Glover on his way in. The party set out early in the morning, sinking at each step knee-deep in the snow. That night they encamped on Bear river. They had believed that they would be able to follow it up, and in this manner avoid the hills. But upon examination, this route was found to be impracticable, in consequence of the river breaking through cañons.

On the 12th, the party resumed their journey, and after traveling about two miles, in snow waist-deep, found it impossible to proceed, and encamped for the purpose of making snow-shoes. The following day, they traveled until noon when they encamped, and spent the afternoon in removing the snow from a *cache* of provisions made by Mr. Reed in the autumn. After digging and melting away thirteen feet of snow, the wagon was found torn in pieces by the grisly bears. The party remained in camp during the 14th, preparing packs and provisions.

On the 15th, they left Bear River valley, in consequence of the immense snow-drifts upon the sides of the ridge, over which the emigrant road passes, from Yuva river to this valley. After traveling fifteen miles, they encamped on the wake of Yuva river. The river was entirely concealed by snow of unknown depth.

The next day, the company proceeded on three miles, when it became necessary to stop and make snow-shoes. On the 17th, after traveling five miles, they encamped on Yuva river, in dry and soft snow fifteen feet deep. They traveled eight miles, on the 18th, and encamped at the head of Yuva river, where the snow was so deep that all the low trees, and of course all the undergrowth, were covered.

February 19.—On the morning of this day, the party resumed its journey. Mr. Glover and Daniel Rhodes became so much exhausted in crossing the Sierra Nevada, that their companions were under the necessity of carrying their packs. After traveling about nine miles, they arrived at The Mountain Camp as the last rays of the setting sun were departing from the tops of the mountains. Every thing was as silent as the grave. A painful stillness pervaded the scene. Upon some of the party raising a shout, for the purpose of finding the cabins, by attracting the attention of the living—if, indeed, any did live—the sufferers were seen coming up out of their snow-holes, from the cabins, which were completely covered, the snow presenting one unbroken level. They tottered toward their deliverers, manifesting a delirium of joy, and acting in the wildest and most extravagant manner. Some wept; some laughed. All inquired, "Have you brought any thing for me?" Many of them had a peculiarly wild expression of the eye; all looked haggard, ghastly, and horrible. The flesh was wasted from their bodies, and the skin seemed to have dried upon their bones. Their voices were weak and sepulchral; and the whole scene conveyed to the mind the idea of that shout having awaked the dead from the snows. Fourteen of their number, principally men, had already died from starvation, and many more were so reduced, that it was almost certain they would never rise from the miserable beds upon which they had lain down. The unhappy survivors were, in short, in a condition the most deplorable, and beyond the power of language to describe, or of the imagination to conceive. The annals of human suffering nowhere present a more appalling spectacle, than that which blasted the eyes and sickened the hearts of those brave men, whose indomitable courage and perseverance, in the face of so many dangers, hardships, and privations, snatched some of these miserable survivors from the jaws of death, and who, for having done so much, merit the lasting gratitude and respect of every man who has a heart to feel for human woe, or a hand to afford relief.

Many of the sufferers had been living for weeks upon bullock hides, and even this sort of food was so nearly exhausted with some, that they were about to dig up from the snow the bodies of their companions, for the purpose of prolonging their wretched lives. Mrs. Reed, who lived in Brinn's cabin, had, during a considerable length of time, supported herself and four children, by cracking and boiling again the bones from which Brinn's family had carefully scraped all the flesh. These bones she had often taken, and boiled again and again, for the purpose of extracting the least remaining portion of nutriment.

Some of the emigrants had been making preparations for death, and at morning and evening the incense of prayer and thanksgiving ascended from their cheerless and comfortless dwellings. Others there were, who cursed God, cursed the snow, and cursed the mountain, and in the wildest frenzy deplored their miserable and hard fate. Some poured bitter imprecations upon the head of L. W. Hastings, for having deceived them as to the road upon which he

had conducted them; and all united in common fears of a common and inevitable death. Many of them had, in a great measure, lost all self-respect. Untold sufferings had broken their spirits, and prostrated every thing like an honorable and commendable pride. Misfortune had dried up the fountains of the heart; and the dead, whom their weakness made it impossible to carry out, were dragged from their cabins by means of ropes, with an apathy that afforded a faint indication of the extent of the change which a few weeks of dire suffering had produced, in hearts that once sympathized with the distressed, and mourned the departed. With many of them, all principle, too, had been swept away by this tremendous torrent of accumulated and accumulating calamities. It became necessary to place a guard over the little store of provisions brought to their relief; and they stole and devoured the raw-hide strings from the snow-shoes of those who had come to deliver them. But some there were, whom no temptation could seduce, no suffering move; who were
"Among the faithless, faithful still."

Upon going down into the cabins of this mountain camp, the party were presented with sights of woe, and scenes of horror, the full tale of which never will be told, and never ought; sights which, although the emigrants had not yet commenced eating the dead, were so revolting, that they were compelled to withdraw, and make a fire where they would not be under the necessity of looking upon the painful spectacle.

On the morning of February 20th, John Rhodes, Daniel Tucker, and R. S. Mootrey, went to the camp of George Donner, eight miles distant, taking with them a little beef. These sufferers were found with but one hide remaining. They had determined, that, upon consuming this, they would dig up from the snow the bodies of those who had died from starvation. Mr. Donner was helpless. Mrs. Donner was weak, but in good health, and might have come into the settlements with Mr. Glover's party, yet she solemnly but calmly declared her determination to remain with her husband, and perform for him the last sad offices of affection and humanity. And this she did, in full view of the fact, that she must necessarily perish by remaining behind.

On the evening of the 20th, the party that had gone down to Mr. Donner's camp in the morning returned, bringing seven persons with them.

The next day, at noon, the party, after leaving all the provisions they could spare, commenced their return from the Mountain Camp to the settlement, with twenty-three persons, principally women and children. The results of the disastrous and horrible journey of Eddy and Foster were carefully concealed from these poor sufferers. To have acted otherwise would have been to overwhelm them with fear and despondency, and this in their condition would have proved fatal.

Mrs. Pike's child and Mrs. Kiesburg's were carried by the party. After proceeding about two miles, two of Mrs. Reed's children gave out; the one a little girl of eight years old, and the other a little boy of four. It became absolutely necessary, therefore, to return them to the Mountain Camp, or to abandon them to die upon the way. The mother was informed by Mr. Glover, that it was necessary to take them back. And now ensued that which it is hoped none may ever be called upon to witness again. She was a wife, and affection for her husband, then in the settlement, no doubt suggested her going on. But she was a mother, also; and maternal love—that strongest of all feelings, that most powerful of all instincts—determined her, immediately, to send forward the two children who could walk, while she would go back with the two youngest, and die with them. It was impossible for Mr. Glover to shake this resolution, although he promised, that when he arrived at Bear River valley, he would go back for them. At length she asked, "Are you, a mason?" Upon receiving an answer in the affirmative she said, "Do you promise me, upon the word of a mason, that when you arrive at Bear River valley, you will return and bring out my children, if we shall not, in the mean time, meet their father going for them?" Mr. Glover replied, "I do thus promise." She then consented to go on. When the mother and children were about to separate, Patty, a little girl eight years of age, took her mother by the hand, and said—"Well, mamma, kiss me. Good-by! I shall never see you again. I am willing to go back to our mountain camp and die; but I can not consent to your going back. I shall die willingly, if I can believe that you will live to see papa. Tell him, good-by, for his poor Patty." The mother and little children lingered in a long embrace. Being separated, Patty turned from her mother to go back to camp. As Mr. Glover and Mr. Mootrey were taking the children back, she told them, that she was willing to go back and take care of her little brother, but that she "should never see mother again." I have given an imperfect sketch of that parting scene; but to do it justice is as impossible as to paint the rainbow, or to throw the sun upon the canvas.

While Mr. Glover and Mr. Mootrey were taking the children back to the Mountain Camp, the company continued to advance, and after proceeding about a mile, encamped at the upper end of Truckee's Lake. This lake, and the river flowing from it, derive their names from an Indian who piloted Mr. Child's company from the sinks of Mary's river to this lake. His name was Truckee, and the emigrants gave his name to the lake and the river. Fremont calls it Snow Lake or Lake Wood. The river is the west fork of Salmon-

Trout river; the east fork heads in Salmon-Trout Lake; and the two unite and flow into Pyramid Lake. There are others in the neighborhood, of great beauty.

Messrs. Glover and Mootrey returned after the party had encamped; but they carefully concealed from Mrs. Reed the fact, that Brinn and wife absolutely refused to permit the children to come into the cabin, until many promises of immediate relief and succor were made. They were even then reluctantly, and with an ill grace, received.

The party were upon an allowance of one ounce of beef and a spoonful of flour, twice per day. The emigrants were almost famished, and some of them that night stole and ate the strings from Mr. Coffeymier's snow-shoes. This circumstance led to an amusing scene, which I would here present, did it not seem to be out of place in a narrative, every page of which presents scenes of horror and sights of woe.

February 22—The company left camp in the morning, crossed the Sierra Nevada, and camped that night at the head of Yuva river. John Denton being missing at the camp, John Rhodes and one other went back and found him in a profound sleep upon the snow. They labored near an hour before they succeeded in rousing him. He was with great difficulty brought up to camp. Here a new misfortune awaited the party. Mr. Glover, upon his going out to the Mountain Camp, had made a *cache* of provisions at this place; but, upon examination, it was found to have been nearly all destroyed by a cougar. This circumstance rendered necessary a further reduction in the daily allowance of food. The effect and consequence of this discovery can not be fully comprehended by persons sitting in comfort, around their firesides, and in the enjoyment of an abundance of the provisions of God's mercy. The poor emigrants wept bitterly, and the stoutest and bravest hearts of those who had gone to rescue them, were not free from fear and despondency.

On the morning of the 23d, Aquilla Glover, R. S. Mootrey, and Edward Coffeymier, hastened forward in advance of the company, for the purpose of obtaining supplies at another *cache*, which had been made at Bear River valley. From this, it was proposed to obtain supplies with which to return to the sufferers. After the company had traveled about one mile, Mr. John Denton became so much exhausted, as to be unable to proceed. He informed his companions, that it was utterly impossible for him to go any further, and stated that they could be of no service to him, and that to remain with him would involve the lives of all. He therefore requested them to leave him, expressing the hope, however, that relief would be sent to him, if possible. They made a fire for him, and after gathering a pile of wood, and leaving with him nearly all the food they had, they left him by the wayside in the wilderness. It will be seen, that Mr. Reed, after this, hurried forward with the hope of rescuing him; but the vital spark had been extinguished in his weary and worn-out body. After Mr. Reed had passed on, Mr. Eddy found him with the provisions still in his pocket.

He was an intelligent and amiable young man about thirty years of age. He was a gunsmith by trade, and was a native of Sheffield, England, where he had a mother living at the time of his last hearing from home. The four years preceding his entering upon this journey, he had resided in Springfield, Illinois, where he left many warmly attached friends. Mr. Eddy had gone back into the mountain for the purpose of taking relief to the emigrants, and found him in a sitting posture, with his body slightly leaning against a snowbank, and with his head bowed upon his breast. He had evidently fallen into a profound slumber, during the continuance of which the circulation had gradually diminished, until he ceased at once to live and suffer, and the transition of his spirit from time into eternity was unperceived.

Mr. Eddy found at his side a small piece of India rubber, a pocket pencil, and a little journal, containing a brief notice of some of the most prominent incidents of the journey, and among others of his Christmas dinner. On a slip of the paper was a piece of poetry, which he had written, making some corrections by rubbing out with his India rubber, and rewriting. It was handed over to Mr. Woodworth, who published it in the "Californian Star." It was written in pencil, and there can be no doubt of his having composed it a little before the coming on of that heavy slumber, from which he will never awake, until the angel Gabriel shall rouse earth's sleeping millions from the grave. When the circumstances are considered in connection with the calamities in which the unhappy Denton was involved, the whole compass of English and American poetry may be challenged to furnish a more exquisitely beautiful—a more touching and pathetic piece. Simple and inornate to the last degree, yet coming from the heart, it goes to the heart. Its lines are the last plaintive notes, which wintry winds have waked from an Æolian harp, the strings of which rude hands have sundered. Bring before your mind the picture of an amiable young man, who has wandered far from the paternal roof, is stricken by famine, and left by his almost equally unhappy companions to perish among the terrible snows of the great Sierra Nevada. He knows that the last most solemn hour is near. Reason still maintains her empire, and memory, faithful to the last, performs its functions. On every side extends a boundless waste of faithless snow. He reclines against a bank of it, to rise no more; and busy memory brings before him a thousand images of past beauty and pleasure, and of scenes he will never revisit. A mother's image presents itself to his mind; tender recollections crowd upon his heart, and the scenes of his boyhood and youth pass in review before him with an unwonted vividness; the hymns of praise and thanksgiving that in harmony swelled from the domestic circle around the family altar are remembered, and soothe the sorrows of the dying man; and finally, just before he expires, he writes—

"O! after many roving years,
  How sweet it is to come
Back to the dwelling-place of youth—
  Our first and dearest home:—
To turn away our wearied eyes
  From proud Ambition's towers,
And wander in those summer-fields—
  The scene of boyhood's hours.

"But I am changed since last I gazed
  Upon that tranquil scene,
And sat beneath the old witch-elm,
  That shades the village green;
And watched my boat upon the brook—
  It was a regal galley,
And sighed not for a joy on earth,
  Beyond the happy valley.

"I wish I could once more recall
  That bright and blissful joy,
And summon to my weary heart
  The feelings of a boy,
But now on scenes of past delight
  I look, and feel no pleasure,
As misers on the bed of death
  Gaze coldly on their treasure."

The party, after providing as far as it was possible for the wants of Mr. Denton, resumed its journey, and after traveling about eight miles in advance, encamped. On that night a child of Mrs. Kiesburg died.

On the morning of February 24th the party resumed its journey, in great weakness, and after traveling within about eight miles of Bear River valley, encamped, and were met by R. S. Mootrey and Edward Coffeymier, with a little beef.

February 25—The company again set out, and after traveling a short distance, met Mr. Reed. Mrs. Reed instantly rushed into her husband's arms. The affecting scene which followed the meeting of the husband and wife, the father and children, it is impossible to describe. The most generous and amiable sentiments of nature and humanity were testified in the joy this unfortunate couple exhibited, when they had sufficiently recovered their senses to realize that they were indeed restored to each other, after so many torturing anxieties, so many cruel misfortunes; and after encountering from their companions a madness so insensate, sustained by a courage the most heroic. They felt and expressed so vividly the happiness they enjoyed in that moment of unsurpassed rapture, that it would have drawn tears from the most obdurate heart.

But other duties and obligations made it necessary for them to separate. There yet remained in this Mountain Camp many who must die, without assistance. Patty was there; and her little brother, a pet of the whole family, was there. These, aside from the peril of other sufferers, appealed to a father's heart to hasten to their rescue.

Mr. Glover's party encamped that night in Bear River valley, where they found their *cache* of provisions undisturbed. Having now a tolerable supply, young Donner ate too much, and was in consequence very sick. Some tobacco juice being given to him to make him vomit, he was well before morning. At breakfast, however, he again ate too much, and died before 10 o'clock.

The company traveled six miles on the 26th, and encamped near the crossing of Bear river.

February 27.—Mr. Glover's party resumed its journey early in the morning, and encamped that night at the Mule Springs, where Mr. Woodworth was encamped on bare ground, the snow being in patches. Horses had been sent from the settlements for the use of the emigrants. After resting over night, such of the sufferers as could ride, were put upon horses; and the party resuming its journey, traveled on to Cache Creek, where it encamped. On the second day of March the sufferers arrived at Johnson's, and finally terminated their laborious, exhausting and fatiguing journey, at Sutter's Fort (Fort Sacramento), on the 4th of March, grateful to Almighty God for His delivering mercy, and to those whom He had honored by making them the instruments of that deliverance.

On the day of the arrival of Mr. Glover's party, at Fort Sacramento, he started back with two of Capt. Sutter's Indians, having ten or twelve horses and six mules loaded with provisions.

They proceeded on to Capt. Kern's camp, about sixty miles from the fort. Here Mr. Glover sent a man (for whom, after inquiring of a number of persons in San Francisco, I could learn no other name than that of "Greasy Jim") forward to Mr. Woodworth, who was in camp at the Mule Spring, about thirty miles distant. Mr. Woodworth sent back the messenger with a note, requesting that the horses should be brought up. Mr. Glover, upon arriving at Mr. Woodworth's camp, met Mr. Reed with Solomon Hook, Patty, and little Tommy.

Mr. Woodworth informed Mr. Glover that Eddy, Foster, and others had gone on, for the purpose of assisting the emigrants, and that it was with difficulty that a party had been obtained. He stated also that he had promised to meet the party of Messrs. Eddy and Foster, with supplies of food; but that his men were not able to go. Messrs. Mootrey and Coffeymier proposed to go, if Mr. Glover would accompany them. These three gentlemen then started, with packs of provisions upon their backs, Mr. Woodworth accompanying them. They traveled eight miles, and halted, about 3 o'clock, P.M., and made a bark shelter for Mr. Woodworth. The next morning, the party again set out, and after traveling six miles encamped at the head of Bear River valley, where a shelter had previously been prepared for Mr. Woodworth. On the following morning, the party resumed its journey, and after traveling twelve miles, encamped at the last Yuva River cañon upon the emigrant road. On the following morning, Messrs. Woodworth, Glover, and Coffeymier set out, and after traveling until about 2 o'clock, halted to make a fire and cook dinner. While thus employed, Mr. Eddy and party met them. Messrs. Woodworth, Glover, Coffeymier, and Mootrey, after dinner, commenced their return toward the settlements, and encamped at the last crossing of Yuva river, at a place where the emigrant road leaves that river. Some time after the fire had been made, Messrs. Foster, Miller, Thompson, and Eddy came up, and encamped. On the following morning, Mr. Woodworth proceeded on, with the gentlemen who were with him.

Here terminates the events connected with Mr. Glover's second expedition. The occurrences from this point properly refer themselves to the account of the expedition of Messrs. Foster and Eddy, whose story will be found.

NICHOLAS CLARK.
1879.

THE FIRST EXPEDITION OF MESSRS. REED AND McCUTCHEON

. . . . . . Farrago libelli.

JUVENAL.

"The miscellaneous subjects of my book."

MR. JAMES F. REED, it will be remembered, had been compelled to leave his company, far back on Ogden's river, on the morning after the unhappy contest with young Snyder. Such was the hostility of the company, with the exception of Milton Elliot and William H. Eddy, to him, that he was not permitted to take a gun, or any other arms, with which to procure game, or to defend himself from savages. After he left camp, Mr. Eddy resolved that he should not be turned upon the road, under circumstances in which he must necessarily perish; and at the hazard of a quarrel with his companions in travel, he followed Mr. Reed, with a gun and some ammunition.

Those who are only conversant with the modes of thought of well-regulated society, will find it difficult to understand the nature and elements of a feeling of hostility, of which the very best men upon the road often become objects. Far removed from the salutary restraining influence which law and the tribunals of justice exert upon even the most profligate and wicked; there being no public opinion in this vast wilderness, a man may have escaped from the gallows, or be a fugitive from the penitentiary, and yet exert an influence, which will finally result in producing a prejudice, and, perhaps, even a positive hostility against men of virtue and intelligence. But there were in Mr. Reed's case some elements of ill-feeling, in addition to those alluded to, which all persons can appreciate. Snyder was one of Mr. Graves' ox-drivers, a daughter of whom he was to marry. This was in itself sufficient to array Mr. Graves and his family, together with all his dependants, and those over whom he could exert an influence, against Mr. Reed. Kiesburg had been required to leave another company, far back on the way, for a great impropriety, often repeated. Mr. Reed was mainly instrumental in that ejection. The divisions and subdivisions of companies, which subsequently took place, had again brought them together in the same company. And now the killing of Snyder, although clearly justifiable, seemed to present an opportunity to Kiesburg for gratifying a deep-seated purpose to be revenged. Accordingly we find that this man, whose character will be more fully exhibited before the curtain falls upon the scenes of this most shocking and revolting tragedy, was the first to propose hanging Mr. Reed, after the arrival of the company, at the evening encampment. This was prevented by the firmness and resolution of Messrs. Eddy and Elliott. Mr. Reed, it will be remembered, left camp on the next morning, leaving his family behind him, to make his way, alone and without food, through a hostile country into the settlements. The history of that journey would, if carefully written, make a volume, every page of which would be replete with instruction and interest. After a thousand hairbreadth escapes, passing through the most terrible scenes, enduring the most cruel sufferings from famine and thirst, struggling with almost inevitable death, and passing days and nights of inexpressible anguish, he finally succeeded, in the good providence of God, in arriving at the settlements.

After recruiting his wasted energies, Mr. Reed obtained provisions and horses, for the purpose of going back to the relief of his family, and the other emigrants. Having passed over the road, after being thrust out by his traveling companions, he knew that they would require assistance, in order to get through. In this enterprise he was assisted by William McCutcheon, who, it will be remembered, had been sent forward with Mr. Stanton from the Salt Lake, to obtain supplies, with which to meet the emigrants. Worn down and exhausted by the journey into the settlements, Mr. McCutcheon did not accompany Mr. Stanton, on his return with two of Captain Sutter's *vaqueros*.

Messrs. Reed and McCutcheon, after obtaining twenty-six horses and mules, with the necessary provisions, and two Indians, from Captain Sutter, set out upon their expedition to cross the mountains. On the second day after leaving Mr. Johnson's, they encountered the snow. On the third day they reached the head of Bear River valley, in two feet snow, with their flour, beef, and beans, in good condition. At this place they found a man, named Jotham Curtis, who had become greatly grieved and vexed with the evil deeds of the uncircumcised Philistines, who had been the companions of his travel. He had fixed upon this spot, as an abiding place, a sort of lodge in the "vast wilderness," in which he might cease to hear of wrong and oppression. But his late companions fully reciprocated the feeling—though, perhaps, even unjustly—which prompted him to desire a separate abode, and, without asking for even a lock of his hair, had hurried forward into the settlement, leaving their afflicted and sorrowing companion to the undisputed possession of his dominions.

He had built a sort of pen, over which he had stretched his tent for a roof. This, in two feet of snow, very imperfectly answered the purpose of a palace for the mountain monarch. Not having any one as yet connected with his establishment to perform the functions of purveyor, he had been reduced to the vulgar necessity of killing and eating his old dog. Upon the whole, Jotham's opinions, like some fruits, had been matured and ripened by frost and snow. In short, his views upon the subject of the blessings of solitude had undergone a most marvelous change, which caused him to determine upon abdicating his sovereignty, on the first suitable occasion. Frost, and hail, and sleet, and snow, had conducted him through a somewhat painful process, to the conclusion that, although a "boundless contiguity of shade" would do well enough for the summer, it was not quite the thing for winter. He was therefore profuse in his thanks to Messrs. Reed and McCutcheon for having come to carry him and his "household" into the settlements. He was informed, however, that they were on their way to their friends and traveling companions, on the eastern side of the mountain; but he was assured that, upon returning, every practicable assistance would be rendered.

Messrs. Reed and McCutcheon resumed their journey the following morning, leaving one Indian and nine head of horses at Jotham's camp, to remain until they returned.

They pursued their way over a difficult mountain, along the emigrant road. Those who subsequently went to the relief of the emigrants avoided this mountain, by continuing up Bear River valley, until they entered the valley of Yuva river. The traveling was so heavy that they were unable to proceed more than three miles, when they encamped in Dry Valley, in three feet of snow. The snow was soft, dry, and very light, and the horses were, in consequence, almost exhausted. The Indian who had accompanied them, became so much discouraged that he secretly left camp to return. His departure being soon discovered, Mr. Reed went back to the camp of Jotham Curtis, who stated that the Indians, after whispering together, suddenly left, about half an hour before; and that they had taken with them three of the horses, which he did not attempt to prevent, because he believed that any effort of that sort would have been useless. The fact was, that Curtis had persuaded them to leave, believing that this would make it necessary for Messrs. Reed and McCutcheon to return, when, he flattered himself, he would be taken out of the snow. Mr. Reed, finding that a further pursuit would be unavailing, returned to his camp in Dry Valley, where he arrived before daylight.

After finishing a hasty breakfast, they resumed their journey for the eastern side of the mountain, along the still ascending ridge between Bear and Yuva rivers. They proceeded, with almost incredible toil, about three miles, when they found the snow four feet deep. They at length arrived at the summit of the ridge, along which they traveled about one mile and a half to a point where they found the snow four and a half feet deep. Here some of the horses becoming exhausted, lay down greatly distressed, with their noses just out of the snow. The saddle-horses were then rode about one mile further, and left; when Messrs. Reed and McCutcheon proceeded on foot for the purpose of ascertaining whether it would be possible to advance. After toiling onward about one mile, the snow was up to their arm-pits. This brought them to the ground which descends towards Yuva river. They now halted to consult. Neither had ever seen snow-shoes. After a few minutes of most anxious and painful deliberation, they resolved to go back. Upon returning to their pack-horses, they found them completely exhausted, and some of them almost smothered in snow. The heads of some were only partially visible; the packs of others were seen a little above the snow, while the head was below. Being at length extricated and taken back into the trail, they were driven to the camp of Jotham Curtis, where Messrs. Reed and McCutcheon arrived at night, suffering greatly from fatigue, and with feelings of the deepest dejection and despondency.

After a very brief rest, Mr. McCutcheon commenced cooking their supper in silence. Mrs. Curtis was unwell and weary. Her husband was dispirited, worn down, and cross as the grisly bear in the forest in which he had made his camp. At length, upon some trifling pretense, he commenced pouring upon Mr. McCutcheon abuse without measure or stint. To all this, however, Mr. McCutcheon gave no attention. His hands were busy with the preparations for the evening meal, and his mind was beyond the mountain. Curtis, however, was rather encouraged by this silence, and his whole conduct was calculated to remind one of a little dog barking at a mastiff. A close observer might indeed have observed, at intervals, the color coming into Mr. McCutcheon's face, and an occasional curl of the brow, which seemed to indicate that it was possible for the little fellow, sitting upon the ground with his toes in the ashes, to get a snap after a while. Mrs. Curtis ventured indeed, once or twice, to hint that neither of the gentlemen were doing any thing wrong, and that herself and husband ought to be very grateful for the deliverance thus brought to them. This, however, only served to increase his wrath, and he made some remarks, amounting to something more than a hint, of his intention to revive in practice an old common-law right, which, although now obsolete, yet was once connected with the marital relation. Mr. McCutcheon, who was a great stalwart Kentuckian, full six feet six inches in height, with a habit of quoting hard names from Shakspeare, as will hereafter be seen, seemed now to be roused into something like a sudden sharp growl, which indicated that he was not in the habit of showing his teeth for nothing; and that he would probably give some little dog a most terrible bite before long.

"Harkee, here, you little mister," said McCutcheon, straightening himself up from over the fire where he had been cooking meat. "Lookee here, I say; if I hear you, you little pictur, saying another word upon that subject, I'll put you on the fire there, and I'll broil you to a cracklin' in two seconds."

Curtis cowered in an instant before the fire of the eyes that flashed upon him; and his wife said, with a trembling voice, that "Jotham meant no harm; he did not intend to do such a thing for any thing in the world—he was only tired, unwell, and a little fretful; but he didn't mean what he said."

"He'd better not," said McCutcheon, as he stooped down again to resume his cooking, "if he don't want me to tear off his arms, and beat him with the bloody ends."

In a short time supper was ready; and McCutcheon said to Mr. Reed, in a whisper, "Reed, ask that starveling, eelskin, snapper, and his wife, to eat of our supper. I don't want to do it; but I know they must be as hungry as wolves. Poor thing, she looks as though she needed food. He's cross, to be sure; but I'd feed Beelzebub, if he was hungry, rather than have him go away and report that a Kentuckian ever turned any one away empty."

"Well, for my part," replied Mr. Reed, with a laugh, "I would not like to have the devil for a guest; but I'll do as you desire."

Mr. Reed then kindly and cordially invited Mrs. Curtis and her husband to partake of the evening meal which had been prepared. The poor woman was hungry, and of course did not decline; but her husband looked sullen, and sat like a spoiled boy in the pouts.

"Why," said McCutcheon at length, as he ran his fingers backward through his long, bushy hair, and looked with well-affected fierceness upon Curtis, "why don't you come to your supper?"

"I—I—I ca—can—can't eat."

"I know better," bellowed McCutcheon, in a voice of thunder. "You're not sick; you can eat; you shall eat. You are as hungry as a wolf. What's the use of being a fool here in the woods. If you don't get right up now, and come here and sit down by your wife, and take hold of your supper, sick or well, I'll take hold of you, and I'll shake you right out of your trowsers in two seconds, you ugly little pictur, you."

This eloquent harangue evidently impressed the mind of Curtis, with the conviction that at least seven evil ones had taken possession of McCutcheon; and deeming it imprudent, at the time, to contend against such odds he acquiesced, and contrived to do most ample justice to the supper.

During the night, when Messrs. Reed and McCutcheon were supposed to be asleep, Curtis commenced bestowing the most abusive epithets upon his wife for having eaten so readily of the supper. She seemed to be half frightened out of her wits, and replied, in a faltering voice, that he knew very well, that at that time, they had not a mouthful remaining of the old dog.

"Reed, Reed!" said McCutcheon, in a low whisper, accompanied with a smart nudge of the elbow in the ribs, "listen to that villainous compound of all that is cowardly, that woman-fighter, that thing, who is so fierce and pugnacious just now. Listen, Reed, she's crying. Shall I get up, and beat him to death? Tell me, quickly!"

"No, no!" replied Mr. Reed. "What will you beat him to death for? Let them alone. It is not probable he will offer any personal violence to his wife?"

"Yes, yes, I know that," said McCutcheon, "but then he's making her cry. It's almost breaking my heart," he continued, as he seemed to be gulping down a sob. "I never could bear to hear a woman cry. And I won't bear it," added he, with an emphatic expletive, and in a voice which had gradually risen from a whisper to a shout.

His actions corresponded with his words; and Curtis, before he expected it, found himself performing sundry feats of ground and lofty tumbling, which finally ended by his finding himself, by some process of legerdemain, in a deep snow-drift, where he was told to remain until it had cooled his wrath.

Curtis at length gathered himself up, and upon coming to the fire, said something about his having fallen among thieves. McCutcheon replied that he had just before fallen into a snow-drift, but that he had previously fallen among the frosts and snows of the Sierra Nevada, where he had been found by a couple of good Samaritans, who were not willing to be called hard names, while they were taking him to an inn. Nor would they permit him to abuse one whom he was under obligation to cherish and protect.

Day at length dawned; the morning meal was prepared, and eaten. Reed and McCutcheon then set about *cacheing* their beef, etc., up in the trees, and the flour in Curtis' wagon, reserving only enough for present use. They then resumed their journey, with all the animals, except a mule that had frozen to death during the night.

After traveling about four miles, they encamped at the foot of the valley. During the night Curtis again became very abusive. No one, however, seemed inclined to notice him, except McCutcheon, who said to Reed, in a whisper, "Reed, Reed! do you hear that fellow again, that starveling, pitiful-hearted Titan, that plague of all cowards, that—"

"Stop, stop," said Reed, amused at his quotations from Shakspeare, and following the example, continued—

" 'breathe awhile,
You tire yourself in base comparisons.' "

"Well, well, I have no patience with him," said McCutcheon. "I have a mind to get up and maul him, until nothing is left of him."

Curtis hearing a whisper, and having a very sensible recollection of the snow drift, observed during the remainder of the night a very becoming silence, and his conduct was otherwise unexceptionable. In the morning, however, he was observed before breakfast to take a firebrand to a place some distance from the camp, as though he was about to make a separate fire. This did not escape the keen eye of the rough and resolute McCutcheon, who immediately went to him, and thundered out a series of his favorite Shakspearian epithets — "You villainous coward! You panderly rascal! You Phrygian Turk! You knave! You — you —"

Here he seemed to have reached the end of his breath, and of his vocabulary at the same moment. But Curtis, anticipating what he would have said, replied, that he was "afeard" of being killed, and that he had gone out there to make a fire.

"Now march right back," said McCutcheon, "and sit down by the fire, and behave yourself, and don't let me know you to make a Judy of yourself any more, or I'll whip you half to death. If it was not for your wife, we would leave you, and trouble ourselves no more with you. But prudence requires us to take you both in together. But you will, I expect, provoke me to give you a most terrible thrashing."

After breakfast, the horses and mules were caught and packed. They resumed their journey, and Curtis pushed forward for the purpose of avoiding the labor of assisting to drive. McCutcheon observed it, and suggested to Reed the propriety of calling back "that unconfinable baseness," as he denominated Curtis. He was permitted to go forward, however; he seemed to hurry on as though he knew that McCutcheon or the pestilence was at his heels. About 10 o'clock, A.M., a pack of goods, owned by Curtis, became loosened, and fell under the mule. This brought McCutcheon's stentorian lungs into full play, in calling Curtis to return. The hills and valleys echoed back the Shakspearian epithets by which he sought to arrest the onward progress of the fugitive. Curtis was driving through the snow at full speed. McCutcheon was behind gaining upon him, and bellowing like "a bull of Bashan." Curtis was in the mean time "booming it," as McCutcheon phrased it, as though he every moment expected to feel the horns. At length, McCutcheon came up with him, and suddenly restored him to hearing, by making some half a dozen very professional applications, not to the organs affected, but to another part, upon the principle of counter-irritation; repeating the application some two or three times on their way back to the mules. As they came within hearing distance McCutcheon called out, "I tell you Reed, he was booming it! The Flemish drunkard—the book of riddles—the mechanical salt-butter rascal—the Banbury cheese—the base Gangorian wight, was going as fast as a race-horse, and was as deaf as an adder, though I bellowed at him like a mad bull, when no more than twenty feet from him."

This little incident having passed off, the party continued on until night, when they encamped. The evening wore away without any thing of much interest occurring. In the morning, after breakfast, they resumed their journey.

After getting out of the snow, Messrs. Reed and McCutcheon gave to Mrs. Curtis and her husband all the food that remained, and then pushed on to Mr. Johnson's, where they arrived in the evening.

JAMES F. REED.

MRS. MARGARET W. REED.

MATTIE J. (PATTY) REED.
(MRS. FRANK LEWIS.)
1854.

VIRGINIA E. REED.
(MRS. J. M. MURPHY.)
1880.

Second Expedition of Messrs. Reed and McCutcheon

About the 22d of February, 1847, Mr. Reed again started from William Johnson's house, with nine men on foot, loaded with provisions. Mr. Eddy wished to accompany him, but such was his weak and feeble condition, that it was not thought safe for him to attempt it. About the 27th February, this party met that of Mr. Glover in Bear River valley, coming out of the snow, at a place where the parties passed in one hour from naked ground to ten feet of snow. Here Mr. Glover informed him that, on the day previous, he had left John Denton at the head of the wake of Yuva river, twenty-five miles distant. That they had gathered for him a pile of wood, and left him with but a very scanty supply of provisions, because they had not more themselves; and that if Mr. Reed would hasten forward he might find him alive. Mr. Reed pressed on; but he was too late; the vital spark had fled. He had died like a lamp which ceases to burn for want of aliment. Without remaining to observe any thing beyond the fact of his decease, a quilt was hastily thrown over him, and the party pursued their journey. About 11 o'clock, A.M., of each day, the snow would become so soft as not to sustain their weight, and this made it necessary for them to remain in camp until midnight, at which time each day's journey was commenced. They thus continued to toil on until March 1st, when they arrived at the Mountain Camp, where they found the emigrants in a most distressing condition.

When Mr. Reed found them, they were in circumstances the most desperate and shocking. He had in the morning sent forward three of his strongest and most active young men, Charles Cady, Charles Stone, and Mr. Clark, with provisions to the Mountain Camp, with directions to distribute the food among those most requiring it, and to remain by them until he came up, for the purpose of preventing them from eating so much as to injure them. The first camp which he reached was that of Mr. Brinn, whom he found with a sufficient supply of provisions, consisting of beef which he had killed when he first made this camp. He had previously consumed all, or nearly all, of his hides. He had, in fact, been more provident in this respect than any of the other emigrants.

At this camp Mr. Reed saw his daughter Patty sitting on the top of the snow with which the cabin was covered. Patty saw her father at some distance, and immediately started to run and meet him. But such was her weakness, that she fell. Her father took her up, and the affectionate girl, bathed in tears, embraced and kissed him, exclaiming, "Oh! papa, I never expected to see you again, when the cruel people drove you out of the camp. But I knew that God was good, and would do what was best. Is dear mamma living? Is Mr. Glover living? Did you know that he was a mason? Oh! my dear papa, I am so happy to see you. Masons must be good men. Is Mr. Glover the same sort of mason we had in Springfield? He promised mamma, upon the word of a mason, that he would bring me and Tommy out of the mountain." Mr. Reed told Patty that masons were every where the same, and that he had met her mother and Mr. Glover, and had relieved him from his pledge, and that he had himself come to her and little Tommy to redeem that pledge, and to take out all that were able to travel.* Mr. Reed, not seeing little Tommy, feared that he was dead. But Patty informed him, as well as her sobs would permit, that he was sleeping. He immediately descended through the snow-hole that led down into the cabin, and found his little boy asleep, and reduced to a mere skeleton. The feelings of the father upon seeing his child in a situation which may not here be described, may be imagined. He woke him up, but the little boy did not recognize him, and would frequently ask Patty, to whom he looked as a sort of mother, if that really was his father. At length he became assured and happy, and seemed to feel that he once more had a protector and friend.

After giving some bread to his own and Mr. Brinn's children, he went to Kiesburg's cabin, about two hundred yards distant, where he found Mr. Stone, who had given to them some refreshments, and was washing the children's clothes. He found them in a most deplorable condition. Mr. Foster's child and Mr. Reed's were in bed, crying incessantly for something to eat. They would stretch out their arms and beg, in the most moving terms and accents, for food. Mr. Stone had already given the children all that he prudently could. But such was the force of the affecting appeal made by these poor, helpless, and unprotected sufferers, that Mr. Reed could not restrain the promptings of his Irish heart, or refrain from giving heed to their cries, and he gave them more, perhaps, than was prudent. Mrs. Murphy, an amiable woman, and the grandmother of Mr. Foster's children, informed Mr. Reed that these children had been in that bed fourteen days. The imagination must fill up the picture.

Messrs. Reed and McCutcheon warmed water, and then divested themselves of their clothing, and left it out upon the snow, in order to avoid becoming polluted with vermin, thoroughly washed the children in soap suds, oiled them, and wrapped them in flannel, and put them to bed in comparative comfort. It is due to Mrs. Murphy to say, that she could not prevent this condition in which Mr. Foster's child and Mr. Reed's were found, for she was herself so reduced by famine, that she was helpless. Mr. Reed was now under the necessity of helping her up. She would sometimes weep, and then again laugh. She was, in short, reduced to childishness. Such, indeed, was the condition of the greatest number.

*It may be proper to mention that the author is not himself a mason.

MEETING OF PATTY AND HER FATHER.

After the children were thus washed, and their wants supplied, Mr. Reed took a kettle of warm water to Kiesburg, and proposed, with the aid of Mr. McCutcheon, to perform the same offices for him. Kiesburg seemed to be greatly moved, and exclaimed in broken English, "Oh, Mr. Reed! is it possible that you have come to wash the feet and body of a poor miserable wretch who once sought to have you hung upon the end of his wagon-tongue? I have so wronged you—have so mistaken your whole character that I can not permit you to do it. Any one but you may do it. This is too much." Mr. Reed said to him that it was an office of humanity, which he was called upon to perform, irrespective of the past; and that oblivion should cover the unhappy scenes and circumstances that had occurred by the way. The men had now, for the first time, a little leisure to observe. The mutilated body of a friend, having nearly all the flesh torn away, was seen at the door—the head and face remaining entire. Half consumed limbs were seen concealed in trunks. Bones were scattered about. Human hair of different colors was seen in tufts about the fire-place. The sight was overwhelming; and outraged nature sought relief by one spontaneous outcry of agony, and grief, and tears. The air was rent by the wails of sorrow and distress that ascended at once, and, as if by previous concert, from that charnel house of death beneath the snow.

Messrs. Reed, Joseph Jaundro, Matthew Dofar, and Hiram Miller then proceeded some eight miles to the camp of Messrs.

Donner; Messrs. Turner, Wm. McCutcheon, and Britton Greenwood, being left with Mrs. Graves, for the purpose of *cacheing*
her few effects, and to have the sufferers in readiness to return
with the party to the settlements.

When Mr. Reed arrived there he found Messrs. Cady and Stone,
who had been sent in advance with provisions to this camp. They
informed him that when they arrived at the camp, Baptiste had just
left the camp of the widow of the late Jacob Donner, with the leg
and thigh of Jacob Donner, for which he had been sent by George
Donner, the brother of the deceased. That was given, but the boy
was informed that no more could be given, Jacob Donner's body
being the last they had. They had consumed four bodies, and the
children were sitting upon a log, with their faces stained with
blood, devouring the half-roasted liver and heart of the father,
unconscious of the approach of the men, of whom they took not the
slightest notice even after they came up. Mrs. Jacob Donner was in
a helpless condition, without any thing whatever to eat except the
body of her husband, and she declared that she would die before
she would eat of this. Around the fire were hair, bones, skulls, and
the fragments of half-consumed limbs. Mr. Reed and party, after
removing the tent to another place, and making Mrs. Donner as
comfortable as possible, retired for the purpose of being relieved
for a brief period from sights so terrible and revolting. They had not
gone far when they came to the snow-grave of Jacob Donner. His
head was cut off, and was lying with the face up, the snow and cold
having preserved all the features unaltered. His limbs and arms had
been severed from the body which was cut open—the heart and
liver being taken out. The leg and thigh which the boy, John
Baptiste, had obtained, had been thrown back, upon the party
coming up with relief. Other graves were seen, but nothing remained in them but a few fragments.

The party then proceeded to the tent of George Donner, who was
in a weak and helpless condition. Mrs. Donner appeared to be
strong and healthy. She would not consent to go, leaving her
husband; and she declined letting her children go, because she said
that she hoped, from what she had learned, that Mr. Woodworth,
would be in camp in a few days, at most, when she thought they
would all be able to go into the settlement. Mr. Cady was in the
mean time sent back to the upper camp with instructions to return
that night with seven days' provisions. After leaving a man to take
care of the sufferers, and to give them their food, Mr. Reed and
party returned to the upper camp, taking two of Jacob Donner's
children, and bringing up a pair of new boots for Kiesburg. After
leaving Mr. Stone to take care of those at this camp, and to give to
them, in proper quantities and at proper intervals, seven days'
provisions, the party set out to cross the mountain.

The following are, in substance, extracts from a journal kept by one of the emigrants, and are introduced here for the purpose of presenting at least an imperfect account of the sufferers in their Mountain Camp. Although it possesses great interest, as showing some of the dire sufferings of the miserable survivors who passed through an ordeal more horrible and terrific than that of either fire or water, yet it must not be regarded as perfect. A multitude of the most shocking and revolting circumstances are designedly suppressed, as being unfit for the sober pages of history. Notwithstanding the unspeakable distress which is known by the world to have existed, and the thrilling scenes which the narrative of this lamentable affair presents, the *full* story will never be told, and the half of that which is known by the people of California will never appear in print; and indeed ought not.

"*Dec.* 17.—Pleasant. William Murphy returned from the mountain last evening. Milton and Noah started for Donner's, eight days ago, and not having returned, it is probable that they are lost in the snow."

"*Dec.* 19.—Snowed last night, but is thawing today, although the wind is northwest."

"*Dec.* 20.—Clear and pleasant. Mrs. Reed is here. We have yet received no account from Milton. Charles Burger set out for Donner's, but was unable to proceed, and turned back. These are tough times, but we are not discouraged for our hope is in God."

"*Dec.* 21.—Milton got back last night from Donner's camp, and brings with him the sad news of the death of Jacob Donner, Samuel Shoemaker, Rianhard, and Smith. The others are in a low situation. The snow fell during the whole of the last night, with a strong southwest wind."

"*Dec.* 23.—Clear to-day. Milton took some of his meat away. All well at their camp. Began this day to read the 'Thirty days' prayers.' Almighty God, grant the request of unworthy sinners."

"*Dec.* 24.—Rained all night, and still continues. Poor prospect for any kind of comfort, spiritual or temporal."

"*Dec.* 25.—Began to snow yesterday. Snowed all night, and it continues to fall rapidly. Extremely difficult to get wood. Offered our prayers to God this Christmas morning. The prospect is appalling, but we trust in Him."

"*Dec.* 27.—Cleared off yesterday, and continues clear. Wood growing scarcer. A tree when felled sinks into the snow, and is hard to get at."

"*Dec.* 30.—Fine, clear morning. Froze hard last night, about ten o'clock."

"*Dec.* 31.—Last of the year. May we spend the coming year better than we have the past. This we purpose to do, if it is the will of the Almighty to deliver us from our present dreadful situation.

Amen. Morning pleasant, but cloudy. Wind east by south. Looks like another snow-storm. Snow-storms are dreadful to us. It is very deep."

"*Jan.* 1, 1847.—We prayed the God of mercy to deliver us from our present calamity, if it be His holy will. Commenced snowing last night, and snows a little yet. Provisions getting very scarce. Dug up a hide from under the snow yesterday, but have not commenced on it yet."

"*Jan.* 3.—Fair during the day. Froze during the night. Mrs. Reed talks of crossing the mountain with her children."

"*Jan.* 4.—Fine morning. Looks like spring. Mrs. Reed and Virginia, Milton Elliott, and Eliza Williams, started a short time ago, with the hope of crossing the mountains. Left their three children here. It was hard for Mrs. Reed to part with them."

" *Jan.* 6. — Eliza came back yesterday, being unable to proceed. The others kept ahead."

"*Jan.* 8.—Very cold this morning. Mrs. Reed and the others came back, not being able to find the way on the other side of the mountain. They have nothing to live on but hides."

"*Jan.* 10.—Began to snow last night, and it still continues. Wind north-northwest."

"*Jan.* 13.—Snowing fast; snow higher than the shanty. It must be thirteen feet deep. Can not get wood this morning. It is a dreadful sight for us to look upon."

"*Jan.* 14.—Cleared off yesterday. The sun shining brilliantly renovates our spirits. Praise the God of Heaven!"

"*Jan.* 15.—Clear day again. Wind northwest. Mrs. Murphy snow-blind. Lanthron not able to get wood. Has but one ax between him and Kiesburg. Looks like another storm. Expecting some account from Sutter's soon."

"*Jan.* 17.—Eliza Williams came here this morning. Lanthron crazy last night. Provisions scarce. Hides our main subsistence. May the Almighty send us help."

"*Jan.* 21.—Fine morning. John Baptiste and Mr. Denton came this morning with Eliza, who will not eat hides. Mrs. _____ sent her back to live or die on them."

"*Jan.* 22.—Began to snow after sunrise. Likely to continue. Wind west."

"*Jan.* 23.—Blew hard, and snowed all night. The most severe storm we have experienced this winter. Wind west."

"*Jan.* 26.—Cleared off yesterday. To-day fine and pleasant. Wind southwest. In hopes we are done with snow-storms. Those who went to Sutter's Fort not yet returned. Provisions getting scant, and the people growing weak, living on a small allowance of hides."

"*Jan*. 27.—Commenced snowing yesterday, and continues to-day. Lewis S. Kiesburg died three days ago. Wood growing so scarce, that we don't have fire enough to cook our hides."

"*Jan*. 30.—Fair and pleasant. Wind west. Thawing in the sun. John and Edward Brinn went to Mr. Graves' this morning. Mr. _____ seized upon Mrs. _____'s goods, to hold them until paid for a little food which she bought. The hides which herself and family subsisted upon were also taken away from her. An opinion may be formed from these facts of the fare in camp. Nothing is to be had by hunting; yet, perhaps, there will soon be."

"*Jan*. 31.—The sun does not shine out brilliantly this morning. Froze hard last night. Wind northwest. Lanthron Murphy died last night, about 10 o'clock. Mrs. Reed went to Graves' this morning, to look after her goods."

"*Feb*. 5.—Snowed hard until 12 o'clock last night. Many uneasy for fear we shall perish with hunger. We have but a little meat left, and only three hides. Mrs. Reed has nothing but one hide, and that is in Graves' house. Milton lives there, and likely to keep that. Eddy's child died last night."

"*Feb*. 8.—It snowed faster last night and to-day than it has done this winter before. Still continues. Wind southwest. Murphy's folks and Kiesburg's say they can not eat hides. I wish we had enough of them. Mrs. Eddy died on the night of the 7th."

"*Feb*. 9.—Mrs. Pike's child all but dead. Milton is at Murphy's, not able to get out of bed. Kiesburg never gets up. Says he is not able. Mrs. Eddy and child were buried in the snow to-day. Wind southeast."

"*Feb*. 10.—Beautiful morning. Thawing in the sun. Milton Elliot died last night at Murphy's shanty. Mrs. Reed went to see after his effects this morning. J. Denton trying to borrow meat for Graves. Had none to give. They had nothing but hides. All are entirely out of meal, but a little we have. Our hides are nearly all eaten up; but, with God's help, spring will soon smile upon us."

"*Feb*. 12.—Warm, thawy morning."

"*Feb*. 14.—Fine morning, but cold. Buried Milton Elliot in the snow. John Denton not well."

"*Feb*. 15.—Morning cloudy until 9 o'clock, then cleared off warm. Mrs. Graves refused to give Mrs. Reed her hides, and to prevent her from getting Sutter's pack-hides to eat, put them upon her shanty."

"*Feb*. 16.—Commenced raining last evening, and then turned to snow in the night, which continued to fall until morning. Weather changeable; sunshine, and then light showers of hail, accompanied by strong winds. We all feel very unwell, and the snow is not getting much less at present."

"*Feb*. 19.—Froze hard last night. Aquila Glover, R. S. Mootrey, Joseph Sell, Daniel Rhodes, John Rhodes, Daniel Tucker, and Edward Coffeymier, arrived from California with provisions, but left the greater part on the way. To-day is clear and warm for this region."

"*Feb*. 20.—John Rhodes, Daniel Tucker, and R. S. Mootrey went to Donner's Camp this morning, and returned this evening, bringing seven persons to go into the settlements. They start to-morrow."

"*Feb*. 21.—To-day, at noon, the party set out with twenty-three of our number, some of them being in a very weak state. Two of Mr. Reed's children brought back."

"*Feb*. 22.—Mrs. Kiesburg started with the Californians yesterday, and left her husband here unable to go. Pike's child died two days ago, and was buried in the snow this morning."

"*Feb*. 23.—Froze hard last night. To-day pleasant and thawy; has the appearance of spring, all but the deep snow. Wind south-southeast. Shot a dog to-day, and dressed his flesh."

"*Feb*. 25.—To-day, Mrs. Murphy says, the wolves are about to dig up the dead bodies around her shanty. The nights are too cold to watch, but they hear them howl."

"*Feb*. 26.—Hungry times. Mrs. Murphy said here yesterday, that she thought she would commence on Milton and eat him. I do not think she has done so yet. It is distressing. The Donners told the California folks six days ago, that they would commence on the dead people, if they did not succeed that day or the next in finding their cattle, then ten or twelve feet under the snow. They did not know the spot or near it. They have done it ere this."

"*Feb*. 28.—One solitary Indian passed by yesterday, coming from the lake. He had a heavy pack on his back, and gave me five or six roots resembling onions in shape, having tough fibers, and tasting something like a sweet potato."

"*March* 1.—Mr. J. F. Reed and nine men arrived this morning from Bear Valley with provisions. They are to start in two or three days, and *cache* our goods here. They say that the snow will remain until June."

The foregoing extracts from a journal kept during the winter, will present some imperfect view of the scenes and events which occurred in the Mountain Camp during the long and dreary winter. But this journal affords only indistinct glimpses of scenes as they passed. The full and complete record of even those circumstances which were entered in that journal were never read by above three persons. They preserve a silence as unbroken as the grave. But many things occurred in that Mountain Camp previous to the first of March, which were not written, except by the recording angel;

and which will never be fully known until God shall bring every secret work into judgment, whether it be good or evil.

After leaving about seven days' provisions with them to sustain them until Mr. Woodworth could come to them with relief, Mr. Reed's party commenced their return to the settlements, with seventeen of the unhappy beings, whose condition during the winter is in part shown by the foregoing journal. These persons were Patrick Brinn, wife, and five children; Mrs. Graves and four children; Mary and Issac Donner, children of Jacob Donner; Solomon Hook, a step-son of Jacob Donner, and two of his children. He had met his wife with two of his children in the Bear River valley.

On the first day they traveled but three miles, although greatly urged by Mr. Reed to go faster and further. They encamped that night on the side of Truckee's Lake. It will scarcely be credited that on this night this company of emigrants, although surrounded by circumstances of extreme peril, amidst the most terrible scenes, and still struggling with death, were in fine spirits, and some of them uttered pleasantries which made their companions smile, notwithstanding the horrors of their condition. Patrick Brinn played about two hours upon a violin, which had been owned by Jay Fosdick, and which Mrs. Graves was taking into the settlements for him, she supposing him to be still living.

On the day that Mr. Reed's party left the camp in Bear River valley, he instructed the men with him not to let the sufferers know any thing in reference to the disasters which befell the party that came in with Mr. Eddy. This was necessary, because of the effects which might, and probably would, have resulted from the depression the communication of the intelligence would have produced.

The night passed away, and in the morning a young man who was carrying $500 in specie for Mrs. Graves, said to one of his companions in a vein of pleasantry, such as that in which they had indulged during the previous night, "I think that we had better play *euchre*, for the purpose of determining who shall have this money." Although nothing was seriously meditated, yet the remark alarmed Mrs. Graves, who, when the company set forward, remained behind for the purpose of concealing the money. Mrs. Graves having perished a few days after this, a knowledge of her secret perished with her.* The party traveled about five miles to the foot of the mountain and encamped, Mr. Reed finding it impossible to induce them to go further. The music of the violin again beguiled the heavily-passing hours. It could not, however, dispel the anxiety which Mr. Reed felt, upon observing a heavy and portentous cloud that hung, with a threatening and vengeful aspect, about the

---

*The money was accidentally found in 1891—Ed.

top of the mountain. Fearing the effects which might result from communicating his apprehensions to any one, he looked in silence upon the gathering storm, which was to sweep with desolating fury and a fearful energy over the sides of the mountains; the pines, standing upon which, seemed even then, as they swayed to and fro in the wind, to be moaning for the dead. After the evening meal, there remained only provisions sufficient to last them one day and a half. On the following morning Mr. Reed sent Joseph Jaundro, Mathew Dofar, and Mr. Turner forward, with instructions to get supplies at a *cache* that had been made about fifteen miles from that place, and to return. If, however, that should be found robbed, they were to go still further on to a second *cache*, unless, in the mean time, they should meet Mr. Woodworth coming to the relief of the sufferers; in which event, they were instructed to return with him as soon as possible. Upon these being sent forward, the party resumed their journey, expecting to meet the supplies thus sent on the next day. They crossed the Sierra Nevada, and after traveling about ten miles, encamped on a bleak point on the north side of a little valley, near the head of Yuva river. During the night a most terrible snow-storm came down upon them, accompanied by a fierce wind, which increased to a tremendous gale before morning. The altitude of the mountain at the pass is 9838 feet. The camp was situated about 1500 feet below, and upon about 40 feet of snow— the snow above being from 60 to 100 feet deep. The storm continued, without the slightest intermission, for two days and three nights. On the morning of the third day the dark and angry clouds gradually passed off, and the air became, if possible, more intensely cold. The sufferings of the party, and especially of the unhappy and emaciated famine stricken emigrants, can never be portrayed with that vividness of coloring which is necessary to convey to the mind an adequate conception of what they endured. It is not possible to present upon the cold, and necessarily imperfect pages of a narrative, a true picture of the distress and anguish of spirit with which this terrible storm overwhelmed them. Individuals who have been so unfortunate as to have been at some times similarly situated, can sympathize, to some extent, with those upon whom it descended with resistless fury. But the more inexperienced reader, sitting in a comfortable parlor, by a cheerful fire, surrounded by happy faces, can never know the suffering of body and tortures of mind, endured by those who felt that they were abandoned by those whose duty it was to come to their relief.

The bleak point upon which they encamped was selected, not from choice, but necessity. Mr. Glover had encamped here on his way to the Mountain Camp, and the snow had in consequence been partially trodden down. It was an object to encamp there, in order to enable the sufferers to keep their feet dry. They had, moreover, traveled ten miles, which, if the feeble condition of the emigrants be considered, will at once be seen to be a hard day's travel, especially so when it is remembered that the party had crossed the mountains. Mr. Glover's party had also left at it some logs; and this, too, was an object with men who, in addition to assisting forward the sufferers during the day, were under the necessity of performing the severest camp duty at night.

The manner in which the fires upon these terrible snows were made by those who were engaged in these expeditions was as follows:—two green logs were cut and laid down at a distance corresponding with the length of the fire necessary to be made. Large green logs of pine or fir were then cut and placed transversely upon the first two. These served as a foundation upon which to build the fire up out of the snow, and upon these the fire was made by piling on dry wood. Boughs were cut down and laid upon the snow around the fire, and upon these the emigrants lay, with their feet to the fire. If the green logs burnt through, the fire fell upon the snow below, and was of course extinguished. Unless, therefore, this could be prevented by putting in other green logs, there was the greatest danger of all perishing with the cold. The heat of the fire above would also sometimes melt the snow below; and if this melting was greater at one end, or upon one side than another, the logs would become displaced, and the fire rolling down into the snow would become extinguished. If the process of melting was uniform, a hole in the snow would thus be made, varying from ten to thirty feet deep.

Such were some of the dangers to which they were exposed during the continuance of this dreadful storm, especially on the third night. Boughs had been set down around the fire. The snow was then thrown from the inside against the boughs, and upon the outside, so as to form a bank to break off the force of the wind and driving snow, which fell so thick as to make it impossible to see beyond a few feet. The cold was so intense as to make it impracticable to chop more than a few minutes without returning to the fire to warm. The party had all lain down, and were seeking to shelter themselves beneath their blankets. The driving snow soon covered them up. Upon some of them rising, the logs were found displaced, and the fire almost extinguished. The men, women, and children, were all so cold as to be in great danger of freezing. Mr. Reed had become snow-blind during the evening, and it was impossible for him to do any thing. The men, with the exception of Hiram Miller, and Wm. McCutcheon, were worn down and disheartened. All became greatly alarmed. The children were all crying. One of the women was weeping—another praying. A portion of Mr. Reed's men were also praying. The two above named were alternately struggling to save the expiring coals, and swearing at the others,

THE BREEN FAMILY.

| 1. PATRICK, SR. | 2. MARGARET. | 3. JOHN. | 4. EDWARD P. | 5. PATRICK, JR. |
| 6. SIMON. | 7. JAMES F. | 8. PETER. | 9. BELLA M. | 10. WILLIAM M. |

urging them to leave off praying and go to work for the purpose of saving the fire; assuring them that all would inevitably perish before morning. Mrs. Brinn's voice was heard above the roaring of the storm, the weeping of the women and children, the prayers of some of the men and the swearing of others. She screamed, "Mr. Rade! Mr. Rade! Do in the name of the blessed Vargin make yer min get up and make a fire. We're all frazin'—every sowl of us! In the name of Saint Patrick and the Vargin, make them get up. They are all gettin' three dollars a day to take us out of the snow, and here they are a-lettin' us all fraze. The Vargin save us! Oh! you've brought us here to murther us! You brought us away from our comfortable camp to fraze us! Oh! Johnny's fell down in the pit and is kilt intirely. Patrick's froze to death. Little Jammy's legs are burnt off by the knees; and Patsy's heart has sased to bate for the space of faftane minutes!" Here Mr. McCutcheon, no longer able to bear this torrent of words, with a multitude of adjectives and expletives, informed her, in a voice he contrived to raise above hers, that if she did not "sase" this abuse and invective, he would, in less time than "faftane minutes," make her heart "sase to bate." The whole scene, though one of distress and the most imminent peril, was one in which the comic and tragical, the terrible and the ludicrous were strangely mingled. At length, however, a fire was made, and it was soon found that Johnny had not been "kilt," nor Patrick froze to death, nor little Jammy "burnt off by the knees," and that Patsy's heart was still "bating," and that Mrs. Brinn's tongue was running with an increased velocity.

Morning came at length, and the storm passed away. The whole party had then been two days without any sort of food. Mr. Reed urged them to resume the journey. None of the party, however, were able to travel except Solomon Hook and Patrick Brinn and family. The latter affirmed that they could remain in camp better without food than travel without it. Mary Donner had burned her foot very much during the previous night, and, although she made an effort, she soon fell, and was assisted back to camp. Mr. Reed and party, after leaving wood for three days, then set out, taking his two children and Solomon Hook, Mr. Miller carried Tom, Solomon Hook also walked. Patty refused to let her father carry her, and continued to travel in the newly fallen snow, into which they all sunk about two feet. Her father frequently asked her if she was not tired or cold, but such was her energy and courage, that she continued to travel on foot, refusing to be carried. At length she called out to her father that she saw the stars and a multitude of angels. He immediately saw that she was freezing, and having wrapped her in a blanket, carried her upon his back. The child derived warmth from the body of her father. The party were all without food, and Mr. Reed had no hope of obtaining assistance from Mr. Woodworth. In fact, he informed the eleven, he had been under the necessity of leaving, that Mr. Woodworth ought to have met them long before, and that to rely upon him any more, was leaning upon a broken stick. The men were very much reduced, from want of food, and worn down by toil. They were, in consequence, greatly discouraged, and expressed their fears that they would all perish; but Patty, who was herself, as has been seen, so near perishing in the morning, said, "No! no! God has not brought us so far to let us perish now." The remark of the child so filled the heart of the rough and resolute McCutcheon, that his eyes immediately filled with tears, that froze as they fell, and he exclaimed, with an oath, "Boys, if there is an angel on earth, Patty is that angel. Just listen to the child." No apology can be made for swearing; and yet the first wish of the heart is, that the tears of the recording angel may have blotted out the oath forever.

Soon after arriving at the encampment, Mr. Stone and Mr. Cady, who had been left at the Mountain Camp, came up. All the men, excepting Mr. Miller and Mr. Stone, found, upon coming to the fire, that their feet were without sensation. Mr. Reed, suspecting that they were frozen, thrust his into the snow, and advised the others to do so. Some of them did it. Mr. Cady, Mr. Dunn, and Mr. Greenwood lost more or less of their toes. Some of them were crippled for life.

The next morning, the party resumed their journey, this being the fourth day they had all been without food. Late in the afternoon, they found a little that had been left in a tree by Mr. Dofar, who had at length, with Mr. Jaundro and Mr. Turner, got forward to a small *cache*. It will be remembered that these men had been sent forward for provisions, when the party arrived at the Starved Camp, where Brinn and his family had been left. The storm, however, had caught these, and they were themselves near perishing. Mr. Turner had been so much frozen, that he was with great difficulty taken forward. They had come to the first *cache*, which they found robbed by wild animals. After the storm abated, they had proceeded on to the second *cache*. A part of this was found, and with it Mr. Dofar had returned, and after depositing it in such a manner as to enable Mr. Reed's party to find it, pursued his way toward Mr. Woodworth's camp.

A little strengthened by this timely supply, the party continued on until night, and encamped. Mr. Cady and Mr. Greenwood had, however, pushed on with the hope of finding Mr. Woodworth. They arrived at his camp after night, I believe, and informed him of the condition of the party. After dark, Woodworth came to Mr. Reed's camp, with Mr. John Starks and Mr. Oakley, the two latter carrying provisions.

This party, finally, after immense toil and extreme peril, arrived in the settlement, without further disaster, or loss of life.

Expedition of Messrs. Foster and Eddy from the California Settlements to the Mountain Camp

THE chapter which I have devoted to showing what were the nature and extent of the preparations made by the people of California for the relief of the sufferers of the Mountain Camp, present the facts which show the manner in which Passed-midshipman S. E. Woodworth became connected with the expeditions for the relief of the emigrants.

Furnished with the most ample supplies, Mr. Woodworth set forward with instructions from Captain J. B. Hull, U. S. navy, and at that time commander of the northern district of California, to use every possible exertion to rescue the unhappy sufferers, agreeing, on the part of the United States, to pay whatever might be necessary to prevent his countrymen from perishing.

Four days after Mr. Woodworth's party left Johnson's ranche, Messrs. Foster and Eddy obtained horses which had been purchased under the order of Captain Hull. With these they set out to meet Mr. Reed and his party.

Mr. Eddy had heard that his wife and one of his children had perished, but he cherished a feeble hope that he was not left to mourn the loss of all; and that he would find one of his children with Mr. Reed; and in any event he felt it to be a duty which he owed to suffering humanity, to do all in his power to rescue others, although his wife and children might be no more. Mr. Foster believed that his child yet survived. He hoped also to find his mother-in-law, Mrs. Murphy, and his brother-in-law, Simon Murphy, alive.

On the second day after they left, they arrived at Bear River valley, where they found Passed-midshipman Woodworth remaining in camp with one man to bring water, make fires, and cook for him. There were also other men in other ways to assist him. Messrs. Eddy and Foster believed that at that time he was over the mountain, and upon inquiring of him why he was not, he replied that he could not go without a guide. Mr. Eddy replied that he had the best guide in the snow trail of those who had preceded him. Mr. Woodworth promised that he would set forward on the following morning, but he advised Messrs. Foster and Eddy not to attempt the passage of the mountain. They informed him that they had passed over under vastly more difficult circumstances, and that they would certainly attempt it again.

They according set out, eight in number, on the following morning. Having crossed a ridge, they arrived at Yuva river, where Passed-midshipman Woodworth, who had become tired from carrying his blanket, proposed, at about 3 o'clock, P.M., to encamp. That night two of Mr. Reed's men came to Mr. Woodworth's camp, and informed him that Mr. Reed's party were encamped about one mile in advance (in the direction of the mountains). Mr. Woodworth then went to Mr. Reed's camp, and after conversing with him, returned. Mr. Reed had informed him that some miles from that place he had left fourteen of the sufferers. Mr. Woodworth asked the men with him, if they would go to the relief of these emigrants, and received a reply in the negative.* Messrs. Foster and Eddy proposed to make themselves responsible for almost any sum to persons who would go with them. To this it was replied that they, having lost all their property and money, were irresponsible. J. F. Reed and Hiram Miller said that they would be responsible for any amount, for which Messrs. Eddy and Foster would engage. But these it was said were in the condition of the first. Mr. John Starks offered to go out without any reward beyond that derived from the consciousness of doing a good act. But the snow made it prudent to have only light men for the service. It was necessary for each man to carry fifty pounds of provisions; and this, added to Mr. Starks' own weight, of two hundred and twenty-four pounds, made it imprudent for him to go.

Being unable to induce any of them to consent to go, Messrs. Eddy and Foster were about to set out alone. Mr. Reed, however, remonstrated against this, and at length induced them to consent to return to Bear River valley, where he said he would use his utmost efforts to prevail upon Mr. Woodworth and his party to enter upon the enterprise. Upon returning to Bear River valley, Mr. Woodworth finally said that he would engage, under the authority he had received from Capt. Hull to pay three dollars per day to every man who would go, and fifty dollars in addition to every man who would bring out a child not his own. Mr. Eddy hired Hiram Miller, formerly of Springfield, Illinois, engaging to pay him fifty dollars.† Mr. Foster hired a Mr. Thompson for the same sum. Howard Oakley, John Starks, and Mr. Stone looked to Capt. Hull for their wages.

The company thus organized, through the instrumentality of Messrs. Eddy and Foster set out for the Mountain Camp, on the following morning. They encamped that night about half way up Yuva river, in fifteen feet of snow. The next day, at 4 o'clock, they arrived at the camp of those whom Mr. Reed had been compelled to leave. The fire at the Starved Camp had melted the snow down to the ground, and the hole thus made was about twelve or fifteen feet in diameter, and twenty-four feet deep. As the snow had

---

*I ought to say here, that in this chapter I omit several facts communicated to me by the emigrants, because I do not wish unnecessarily to involve myself in a newspaper controversy with others, and because their omission does not affect the fidelity of a narrative, having for its object the showing of how and in what numbers the sufferers were rescued.—Author.

†During my sojourn in California, I saw this debt paid.

continued to melt, they made steps by which they ascended and descended.

The picture of distress which was here presented, was shocking indeed. And yet Patrick Brinn and his wife seemed not in any degree to realize the extent of their peril, or that they were in peril at all. They were found lying down sunning themselves, and evincing no concern for the future. They had consumed the two children of Jacob Donner. Mrs. Graves' body was lying there with almost all the flesh cut away from her arms and limbs. Her breasts were cut off, and her heart and liver taken out, and were all being boiled in a pot then on the fire. Her little child, about thirteen months old, sat at her side, with one arm upon the body of its mangled mother, and sobbing bitterly, cried, Ma! ma! ma! It was a helpless and innocent lamb among the wolves of the wilderness. Mr. Eddy took up its wasted form in his arms, and touched even to tears with the sight he witnessed, he kissed its wan and pale cheeks again and again; and wept even more bitterly in the anguish of his spirit as he thought of his own dear ones, and the departed companion of his perils and sorrows. The child looked up imploringly into his face, and with a silent but expressive eloquence, besought him to be its protector. In a few minutes it nestled in his bosom, and seemed to feel assured that it once more had a friend. As soon as possible, he made some thin soup for the infant, which revived it, and, with the exception of an occasional short convulsive sob or sigh, it again appeared quiet and happy. It was brought safely into the settlements, where its very misfortunes made friends for it. But it drooped and withered away like a flower severed from the parent stem. It now blooms in the paradise of God, in a better and happier clime, where the storms and disasters of life will affect it no more.

After supplying these emigrants with food, Messrs. Oakley, Starks, and Stone were left to lead them on to Bear River valley, and to carry out Mrs. Graves' babe and two other children. Messrs. Eddy, Foster, Thompson, and Miller, started at about 4 o'clock, on the following morning, for the Mountain Camp, where they arrived at about 10 o'clock, A.M.

A more shocking picture of distress and misfortune, can not be imagined, than the scene they witnessed upon their arrival. Many of those who had been detained by the snows had starved to death. Their bodies had been devoured by the wretched survivors; and their bones were lying in and around the camps. A body with half the flesh torn from it, was lying near the door. Upon turning over a head which was severed from the body, Mr. Eddy instantly recognized the familiar face of an old friend and traveling companion. A dead child lay near. The wild, fiery, and fierce look of the eyes, and the emaciated and ghastly appearance of the survivors added tenfold horror to this scene of the Mountain Camp.

It is impossible for human language to describe the change wrought in the feelings of those who, but a few weeks before, would have preferred a thousand deaths to eating human flesh. The change which their unspeakable sufferings had produced seemed to affect the very texture of their nature and being. In the solitude and horror of the Mountain Camp, long nights of physical suffering and mental anguish had succeeded each other, in a manner of which it is impossible to have an adequate idea. Days had followed each other in a long succession; but no sun of hope had arisen to dispel the darkness of their misery; and as the long nights came on, the yet driving snow was heaped in impenetrable drifts above them, and extinguished even the dim rays which had sometimes shone fitfully through the dark clouds of disaster, which seemed to be fast thickening, and settling down upon them in a night of death. Surmisings had often been indulged, as to their probable fate; and questions had been asked for the thousandth time, as to the probabilities of relief. They had made calculations for the next and succeeding meals, as they sat gloomily around the fires of their miserable camps. Some had added the last little fuel to the dim and flickering flame, and had given themselves up to the ravings of despair and madness, as they felt the crush of their reliance for aid from the settlements. Others had bowed their heads in moody silence upon the palms of their hands, and given themselves up to the tortures of thought. Here and there one was found, in whose face meekness and resignation were visible, and they seemed to say, "Father, not my will, but thine be done."

Day after day had passed away, and the scanty store of food, miserable and loathsome as it was, had rapidly diminished, until the last hide had been consumed. Then hunger, keen, gnawing, and maddening, preyed upon them, until it might have been said of those who unlike some of their more miserable companions, had up to that time refrained from eating human flesh, "In their gloomy looks you might see the longings of the cannibal." Many expedients had been discussed, for the purpose of avoiding the dreadful alternative of dying themselves, or of killing their companions, by lot or otherwise, to preserve their own lives. But at that juncture a greater number of persons perished from famine, than was necessary to supply, for a time, all the miserable survivors with this horrible food.

It is said that, immediately previous to this, a sacrifice had been agreed upon, and that an individual, who was supposed to have less claims to life than the others, had been selected as the victim. But Providence interposed, and some of them sank into the arms of death, whispering praise for unmerited mercies; while others expired, cursing their miserable fate. And now those who, but a short time before, would have shuddered at the thought of devouring the dead bodies of their companions, rejoiced at their decease, and regarded it as a providential interference in their behalf.

In a very brief period, all the fountains of the heart's purest, noblest, and best affections were dried up, and in some instances every tie was sundered by the one great absorbing thought of individual self-preservation, which led them to escape, if possible, and without regard to others, from the calamities surrounding them.

Something was absolutely necessary to be done to sustain their miserable existence; yet all of them, except Kiesburg, had refrained from this most monstrous food as long as any thing else could be had. Once, when the snows had partially melted away, and the emigrants were enabled to find four hides and a dead bullock, upon which this man, as did the other emigrants, might have subsisted for a time, he took a child of Mr. Foster's, aged about four years, and devoured it before morning. What adds, if possible, to the horror of this horrible meal, is the fact that the child was alive when it was taken to bed; leading to the suspicion that he strangled it, although he denies this charge. This man also devoured Mr. Eddy's child, before noon on the next day, and was among the first to communicate the fact to him. When asked by the outraged father why he did not eat the hides and bullock, he coolly replied, that he preferred human flesh, as being more palatable, and containing more nutriment.

Such was the horrible and emaciated appearance of this man that Mr. Eddy, as he informed me, could not shed his blood there; but he resolved to kill him upon his landing at San Francisco, if he ever came to the place. Mr. Eddy subsequently armed himself for that purpose, but was prevented by Mr. J. F. Reed and Edwin Bryant, Esq., the author of "What I saw in California."

I would without hesitancy express the opinion, that Kiesburg was at the time insane, had he not, long after his subsequent arrival in the settlements of California, shown himself to be a wild beast, by declaring with a profane expletive, that "A man is a fool who prefers poor California beef to human flesh." But the closing scenes of the Mountain Camp will more fully show that this man is perhaps without a parallel in history.

Whatever may be our feelings toward Kiesburg, we should not censure others who were already overwhelmed with misfortunes, but pity their condition, rather than cherish indignation against them for doing that which they could not avoid. We should rather shed tears of sorrow and sympathy for those who were reduced to such dreadful extremities, that their own lives could only be preserved by devouring the bodies of their companions. It will be impossible to prevent some share of our indignation from being directed against those who, by inducing the emigrants to leave the usual route, were the causes of their misfortunes.

The party of Messrs. Eddy and Foster, upon their arrival at the Mountain Camp, found five living children, to wit: three of George Donner's, one of Jacob Donner's, and one of Mrs. Murphy's. They also found a man whose name is Clarke. He was a shoemaker. He had been a sailor also, and I believe he ran away from the ship. I mention these particulars that he may not be confounded with a worthy gentleman of the same name in San Francisco, with whom I traveled upon a part of my journey to Oregon.

Clarke had gone out with Mr. Reed, I believe, under the pretense of assisting the emigrants. He was found with a pack of goods upon his back, weighing about forty pounds, and also two guns, about to set off with his booty. This man actually carried away this property, which weighed more than did a child he left behind to perish. But this is not the only instance of the property of emigrants in distress being appropriated under some pretense, or directly stolen by thieves who prowled about the camp.

In addition to these, there were in camp, Mrs. Murphy, Mr. and Mrs. George Donner, and Kiesburg—the latter, it was believed, having far more strength to travel than others who had arrived in the settlements. But he would not travel, for the reason, as was suspected, that he wished to remain behind for the purpose of obtaining the property and money of the dead.

Mrs. George Donner was in good health, was somewhat corpulent, and certainly able to travel. But her husband was in a helpless condition, and she would not consent to leave him while he survived. She expressed her solemn and unalterable purpose, which no danger and peril could change, to remain, and perform for him the last sad offices of duty and affection. She manifested, however, the greatest solicitude for her children; and informed Mr. Eddy that she had fifteen hundred dollars in silver, all of which she would give to him, if he would save the lives of the children. He informed her that he would not carry out one hundred dollars for all that she had, but that he would save the children, or perish in the effort.

The party had no provisions to leave for the sustenance of these unhappy and unfortunate beings. After remaining about two hours, Mr. Eddy informed Mrs. Donner that he was constrained by the force of circumstances to depart. It was certain that George Donner would never rise from the miserable bed upon which he had lain down, worn out by toil, and wasted by famine. It was next to absolutely certain, if Mrs. Donner did not leave her husband, and avail herself of the opportunity then presented for being conducted into the settlement, that she would perish by famine, or die a violent death at the hands of a cannibal. The instinct of a mother strongly urged her to accompany her children, that she might be able to contribute her own personal efforts and attention to save the lives of her offspring. The natural love of life, too, was without doubt then felt, urging her to fly from a scene of so many horrors and dangers. Her reason, may have asked the question, ''Why remain in the midst of so much peril, and encounter an inevitable death—a death of all others the most terrible—since it is certain that nothing can rescue your husband from the jaws of the all-devouring grave? and when you can not hope to do more than beguile, with your society, presence, and converse the solitude of the few hours that remain of a life, the flame of which is already flickering, and must in a very brief period be extinguished in the darkness and gloom of death?''

A woman was probably never before placed in circumstances of greater or more peculiar trial; but her duty and affection as a wife triumphed over all her instincts and her reason. And when her husband entreated her to save her life and leave him to die alone, assuring her that she could be of no service to him, since he probably would not survive, under any circumstances, until the next morning, she bent over him, and with streaming eyes kissed his pale, emaciated, haggard, and even then death-stricken cheeks, and said:—

''No! no! dear husband, I will remain with you and here perish, rather than leave you to die alone, with no one to soothe your dying sorrows, and to close your eyes when dead. Entreat me not to leave you. Life, accompanied with the reflection that I had thus left you, would possess for me more than the bitterness of death; and death would be sweet with the thought, in my last moments, that I had assuaged one pang of yours in your passage into eternity. No! no! this once, dear husband, I will disobey you! No! no! no!'' she continued, sobbing convulsively.

The parting scene between the parents and children is represented as being one that will never be forgotten, as long as reason remains, or memory performs its functions. My own emotions will not permit me to attempt a description, which language, indeed, has not the power to delineate. It is sufficient to say that it was affecting beyond measure; and that the last words uttered by Mrs. Donner, in tears and sobs, to Mr. Eddy, were, ''O, save! save my children!''

Mr. Eddy carried Georgiana Donner, who was about six years old; Hiram Miller carried Eliza Donner, about four years old; Mr. Thompson carried Frances Ann Donner, about eight years old; William Foster carried Simon Murphy, eight years old; and Clarke carried his booty, and left a child of one of the Donners to perish.

The first night after leaving the Mountain Camp, the party encamped at the foot of the pass, on the eastern declivity of the mountain. On the next day they crossed the pass, where Mr. Eddy found an aperture in the snow which had been kept open by a spring, where, by letting down a cord, he ascertained the depth of the snow to be sixty-five feet. That night they encamped half way down Yuva river. The next morning, they resumed their journey, and came up with Mr. Starks, with Patrick Brinn and family, and others, who were the eleven persons that remained alive of the fourteen whom Mr. Reed had been constrained to leave. They at the same time met Messrs. Glover, Coffeymier, Mootrey, and Woodworth, who had halted to prepare dinner. After the meal was taken, these gentlemen set out for the Mule Spring.

Toward the close of the afternoon, Mr. Woodworth's party encamped at the last crossing of Yuva river. At night Messrs. Eddy, Foster, Thompson, and Miller came up, bringing with them the children with whom they had left the Mountain Camp. John Baptiste and Clarke were also with them. Here they encamped in the snow.

On the following morning, Mr. Woodworth gave to the party a little food. He was informed that there were persons yet remaining at the Mountain Camp, for whose rescue an effort ought to be made. He replied, that he could not remain any longer, and after giving his blankets to Mr. Mootrey to carry, he said he would go forward and prepare horses for proceeding immediately on into the settlements. Messrs. Woodworth, Glover, Mootrey, and Coffeymier then proceeded forward to the Mule Spring, where they encamped.

Messrs. Foster, Eddy, Miller, and Thompson resumed their journey, and at 10 o'clock, A.M., arrived at the Mule Spring. Here they came up with Messrs. Oakley and Stone, who, having left Mr. Starks, had passed Messrs. Foster, Eddy, Miller, and Thompson.

On the evening of the second day after their arrival at this camp, Mr. Starks came up, with Patrick Brinn, his wife, and children. Mr. Starks carried Jonathan Graves, a boy twelve years of age.

Mr. Stone had carried the deceased Mrs. Graves' babe. Mr. Oakley carried Mary Donner, a girl thirteen years old, one of whose feet had been severely burnt at the Starved Camp, previous to Mr. Reed leaving at that place the fourteen, as previously mentioned.

The morning following the day upon which Mr. Starks came up, the whole number of persons thus brought together set out for the settlements; and in three days arrived at Fort Sacramento, the residence of Capt. Sutter.

EXPEDITION OF MESSRS. STARK AND OTHERS

IT will be remembered that Messrs. Starks, Stone, Oakley, Thompson, Miller, Foster, and Eddy, when on their way from the Mountain Camp, with a company of the sufferers, met Messrs. Woodworth, Glover, Mootrey, and Coffeymier, and that Mr. Woodworth was informed that there yet remained several persons at the Mountain Camp, for whose rescue an effort ought to be made.

From the point at which this information had been communicated, Mr. Glover proceeded on to Fort Sacramento, where he saw Mr. McKinstry, and informed him that Mr. Woodworth had declined making any further efforts to have the emigrants rescued. Mr. McKinstry promised to send a letter to Mr. Woodworth, urging him to send a party out. Mr. Woodworth received this letter March 23d. He then organised a party, consisting of John Rhodes, John Starks, E. Coffeymier, John Sel, Daniel Tucker, William Foster, and the son of Mrs. Graves; who were dispatched with provisions and horses.

This party proceeded no further than Bear River valley, or the foot of the mountain, from which point they returned, in consequence of the snow upon the mountain having become so soft, as to make the traveling impracticable.

C. T. STANTON.
1844.

WILLIAM McCUTCHEN.
1880.

LEWIS KEESBERG
1879

MR. FELLUN'S EXPEDITION

MR. FELLUN set out from the settlements in April, with six others, for the relief of such persons as might be found to survive at the Mountain Camp; and also to collect and, as far as practicable, secure the scattered property of both the living and the dead.

Upon arriving at the Mountain Camp, he found that all had perished except Kiesburg. A perusal of the following extract from Mr. Fellun's journal, as published in the California Star upon his return, is well calculated to create a painful suspicion, that this man remained at the Mountain Camp, to appropriate the property and money of the dead, and that he killed Mrs. Donner, Mrs. Murphy, and the child which the man Clark left there to perish. But this is not the only instance of the property of emigrants in distress being appropriated. Almost all which the perils and dangers of my own journey had left to me, in going into Oregon, was taken by a needy adventurer, who had come from the settlements, and had united with another, distinguished for even less principle than himself.

Mr. Fellun says:—

"Left Johnson's on the evening of April 13th, and arrived at the lower end of the Bear River valley on the 15th. Hung our saddles upon the trees, and sent the horses back, to be returned again in ten days, to bring us in again. Started on foot, with provisions for ten days, and traveled to the head of the valley, and camped for the night; snow from two to three feet deep. Started early in the morning of the 15th, and traveled twenty-three miles; snow ten feet deep.

"*April* 17.—Reached the cabins between 12 and 1 o'clock. Expected to find some of the sufferers alive, Mrs. Donner and Kiesburg, in particular. Entered the cabins, and a horrible scene presented itself—human bodies terribly mutilated, legs, arms, and skulls, scattered in every direction. One body, supposed to be that of Mrs. Eddy, lay near the entrance, the limbs severed off, and a frightful gash in the skull. The flesh was nearly consumed from the bones, and a painful stillness pervaded the place. The supposition was, that all were dead, when a sudden shout revived our hopes, and we flew in the direction of the sound. Three Indians, who had been hitherto concealed, started from the ground and fled at our approach, leaving behind their bows and arrows. We delayed two hours in searching the cabins, during which we were obliged to witness sights from which we would have fain turned away, and which are too dreadful to put on record. We next started for Donners' camp, eight miles distant over the mountains. After traveling about half way, we came upon a track in the snow which excited our suspicion, and we determined to pursue it. It brought us to the camp of Jacob Donner, where it had evidently left that morning. There we found property of every description, books, calicoes, tea, coffee, shoes, percussion caps, household and kitchen furniture, scattered in every direction, and mostly in the water. At the mouth of the tent stood a large iron kettle, filled with human flesh, cut up. It was from the body of George Donner. The head had been split open, and the brains extracted therefrom, and, to the appearance, he had not been long dead—not over three or four days, at the most. Near by the kettle stood a chair, and thereupon three legs of a bullock that had been shot down in the early part of the winter, and snowed upon before it could be dressed. The meat was found sound and good, and, with the exception of a small piece out of the shoulder, wholly untouched. We gathered up some property, and camped for the night.

"*April* 18.—Commenced gathering the most valuable property, suitable for our packs, the greater portion requiring to be dried. We then made them up, and camped for the night.

"*April* 19.—This morning, Foster, Rhodes, and J. Foster, started, with small packs, for the first cabins, intending from thence to follow the trail of the person that had left the morning previous. The other three remained behind to *cache* and secure the goods necessarily left there. Knowing the Donners had a considerable sum of money, we searched diligently, but were unsuccessful. The party for the cabins were unable to keep the trail of the mysterious personage, owing to the rapid metling of the snow; they, therefore, went direct to the cabins, and, upon entering, discovered Kiesburg lying down amidst the human bones, and beside him a large pan full of fresh liver and lights. They asked him what had become of his companions; whether they were alive; and what had become of Mrs. Donner. He answered them by stating that they were all dead. Mrs. Donner, he said, had, in attempting to cross from one cabin to another, missed the trail, and slept out one night; that she came to his camp the next night, very much fatigued; he made her a cup of coffee, placed her in bed, and rolled her well in the blankets; but the next morning found her dead. He ate her body, and found her flesh the best he had ever tasted. He further stated, that he obtained from her body at least four pounds of fat. No traces of her person could be found, nor of the body of Mrs. Murphy either. When the last company left the camp, three weeks previous, Mrs. Donner was in perfect health, though unwilling to come and leave her husband there, and offered $500 to any person or persons who would come out and bring them in—saying this in the presence of Kiesburg—and that she had plenty of tea and coffee. We suspected that it was she who had taken the piece from the shoulder of beef in the chair before mentioned. In the cabin with Kiesburg were found two kettles of human blood, in all supposed to be over one gallon. Rhodes asked him where he had got the blood. He answered, "There is blood in dead bodies." They asked him numerous questions, but he appeared embarrassed, and equivocated a great deal; and in reply to their asking him where Mrs. Donner's money was, he evinced confusion, and answered, that he knew nothing about it—that she must have *cached* it before she died. 'I hav'n't it,' said he, 'nor the money, nor the property of any person, living or dead!' They then examined his bundle, and found silks and jewelry, which had been taken from the camp of the Donners, amounting in value to about $200. On his person they discovered a brace of pistols, recognized to be those of George Donner, and, while taking them from him, discovered something concealed in his waistcoat, which on being opened was found to be $225, in gold.

"Before leaving the settlements, the wife of Kiesburg had told us that we would find but little money about him; the men, therefore, said to him, that they knew he was lying to them, and that he was well aware of the place of concealment of the Donners' money. He declared, before heaven, he knew nothing concerning it, and that he had not the property of any one in his possession. They told him, that to lie to them would effect nothing; that there were others back at the cabins, who, unless informed of the spot where the treasure was hidden, would not hesitate to hang him upon the first tree. Their threats were of no avail; he still affirmed his ignorance and innocence. Rhodes took him aside and talked to him kindly, telling him, that if he would give the information desired, he should receive from their hands the best of treatment, and be in every way assisted; otherwise, the party back at Donners' camp would, upon its arrival, and his refusal to discover to them the place where he had deposited this money, immediately put him to death. It was all to no purpose, however, and they prepared to return to us, leaving him in charge of the packs, and assuring him of their determination to visit him in the morning; and that he must make up his mind during the night. They then started back and joined us at Donners' camp.

"*April* 20.—We all started for Bear River valley, with packs of one hundred pounds each; our provisions being nearly consumed, we were obliged to make haste away. Came within a few hundred yards of the cabin which Kiesburg occupied, and halted to prepare breakfast, after which we proceeded to the cabin. I now asked Kiesburg if he was willing to disclose to me where he had concealed that money. He turned somewhat pale, and again protested his ignorance. I said to him, 'Kiesburg, you know well where Donner's money is, and d - - n you, you shall tell me! I am not going to multiply words with you, or say but little about it; bring me that rope!' He then arose from his pot of soup and human flesh and begged me not to harm him; he had not the money nor the goods; the silk clothing and money which were found upon him the previous day, and which he then declared belonged to his wife, he now said were the property of others in California. I then told him I did not wish to hear more from him, unless he at once informed us where he had concealed the money of those orphan children; then producing the rope, I approached him. He became frightened; but I bent the rope about his neck, and threw him, after a struggle, upon the ground, and as I tightened the cord, and choked him, he cried out that he would confess all upon release. I then permitted him to arise. He still seemed inclined to be obstinate, and made much delay in talking; finally, but with evident reluctance, he led the way back to Donners' camp, about ten miles distant, accompanied by Rhodes and Tucker. While they were absent, we moved all our packs over to the lower end of the lake, and made all ready for a start when they should return. Mr. Foster went down to the cabin of Mrs. Murphy, his mother-in-law, to see if any property remained there worth collecting and securing; he found the body of young Murphy, who had been dead about three months, with the breast and skull cut open, and the brains, liver, and lights taken out; and this accounted for the contents of the pan which stood beside Kiesburg, when he was found. It appears that he had left at the other camp the dead bullock and horse, and on visiting this camp and finding the body thawed out, took therefrom the brains, liver, and lights

"Tucker and Rhodes came back the next morning, bringing $273, that had been *cached* by Kiesburg, who after disclosing to them the spot, returned to the cabin. The money had been hidden directly underneath the projecting limb of a large tree, the end of which seemed to point precisely to the treasure buried in the earth. On their return, and passing the cabin, they saw the unfortunate man within, devouring the remaining brains and liver, left from his morning repast. They hurried him away, but before leaving, he gathered together the bones and heaped them all in a box he used for the purpose, blessed them and the cabin, and said, 'I hope God will forgive me what I have done; I couldn't help it! and I hope I may get to heaven yet!' We asked Kiesburg why he did not use the meat of the bullock and horse instead of human flesh. He replied, he had not seen them. We then told him we knew better, and asked him why the meat in the chair had not been consumed. He said, 'Oh, it's too dry eating! the liver and lights were a great deal better, and the brains made good soup!' We then moved on, and camped on the lake for the night.

"April 21.—Started for Bear River valley this morning; found the snow from six to eight feet deep; camped on Yuva river for the night. On the 22d, traveled down Yuva about eighteen miles, and camped at the head of Bear River valley. On the 25th, moved down to the lower end of the valley; met our horses, and came in.''

The last of the survivors of the Mountain Camp had now been brought in. The following list presents the names of the party. Those who perished were:—C. T. Stanton; Mr. Graves; Mrs. Graves; Franklin Graves; Jay Fosdick; John Denton; George Donner; Mrs. Donner, his wife; Jacob Donner; Betsy Donner; Isaac Donner; Lewis Donner; Samuel Donner; Charles Burger; Joseph Rianhart; Augustus Spitzer; Samuel Shoemaker; James Smith; Baylis Williams; Bertha Kiesburg; Lewis S. Kiesburg; Mrs. Murphy; Lemuel Murphy; Lanthron Murphy; George Foster; Catharine Pike; William Pike; Eleanor Eddy; Margaret Eddy; James Eddy; Patrick Dolan; Milton Elliott; Lewis and Salvadore, Capt. Sutter's vaqueros.—In all (including two who died before reaching the Mountain Camp) 36.

The following survived:—William Graves; Mary Graves; Ellen Graves; Viney Graves; Nancy Graves; Jonathan Graves; Elizabeth Graves; Sarah Fosdick; Loithy Donner; Leon Donner; Frances Donner; Georgiana Donner; Eliza Donner; George Donner, Jun.; Mary Donner; John Baptiste; Solomon Hook; Mrs. Wolfinger; Lewis Kiesburg; Mrs. Kiesburg; William Foster; Sarah Foster; Simon Murphy; Mary Murphy; Harriet Pike; Miriam Pike; Patrick Brinn; Margaret Brinn; John Brinn; Edward Brinn; Patrick Brinn, Jun.; Simon Brinn; James Brinn; Peter Brinn; Isabella Brinn; Eliza Williams; Noah James; James F. Reed; Mrs. Reed; Virginia Reed; Patty Reed; James Reed; Thomas Reed; William H. Eddy.—In all, 44.

The following Table exhibits the sex of those who were lost, and of those who were saved:—

	Males.	Females.	Total.
Number who perished	28	8	36
" " survived	20	24	44
Total	48	32	80
Number who perished.	28	8	
Had the rate of mortality in the sexes been equal there would have died .	$21\frac{3}{5}$	$14\frac{2}{5}$	
Dif. against males, and in favor of females	$6\frac{2}{5}$	$6\frac{2}{5}$	

THE SENSATIONS AND MENTAL CONDITIONS OF THE SUFFERERS

I WILL now make some remarks, in addition to those already made, respecting the sensations of the sufferers, and their mental condition, as far as I have been able to obtain information from the survivors, or to infer it from the events narrated.

Some of the unfortunate sufferers entirely lost their reason. Of this number was Patrick Dolan, at the Camp of Death. His words were vague and unconnected. He struggled until he got out from under the blankets. He called to Mr. Eddy, saying that he was the only person of their number who could be depended upon. He then pulled off his boots, and, divesting himself of nearly all his clothing, he bade Mr. Eddy follow him, and said that they would be in the settlements in a few hours. He was with great difficulty brought under the blankets, and held there until at length he became as quiet and submissive as a child; when he soon expired, as though he was in a calm and pleasant sleep.

Lanthron Murphy was of this number also.

Mr. Foster was likewise insane; but his was an insanity which, though complete, was of a totally different character. He, in a considerable degree, realized his situation, and in some respects was capable of reasoning from cause to effect. Nevertheless, his mental condition was one which rendered him irresponsible for his actions. His conduct as exhibited in the account of the journey of the sixteen from the Mountain Camp, is not in any degree in keeping with his general character, both before he entered upon this journey, and since his arrival in San Francisco, where he now resides, and is esteemed a reputable and worthy man.

Mr. Eddy was probably the only really sane one of that party of sixteen.

With but few exceptions, all the sufferers, both those who perished and those who survived, manifested the same species of insanity as did Mr. Foster.

Objects delightful to the senses often flitted across the imagination; and a thousand phantasies filled and disturbed the disordered brain. Of this number I may mention the unhappy Denton, who, however, was sometimes perfectly sane; and was undoubtedly so when he finally perished. But the whole number, with very few exceptions, might be individually named as examples.

Their deluded fancies often represented to them during the day, beautiful farm-houses and extensive fields and gardens in the distance. Toward these they pressed forward with all the energy with which alternate hope and despair could inspire them. During the night they often heard men talking, dogs barking, cocks crowing, and bells tinkling. These cruel mockings were probably the effects of fever. Many believed that they were surrounded by familiar faces and old friends; and that they saw objects associated with scenes of other years and places. Some saw persons coming to their relief, and called to them to hasten. Many fancied, although in the midst of winter, that they were traveling through highly cultivated regions in the midst of harvest. There were instances of persons suspecting at times that the circumstances with which they were surrounded were not real; and that they were deceived by the illusions of the most horrible dreams, and they would rub their eyes and put their hands upon the head for the purpose of assuring themselves, if possible, that all was not the result of a dreadful vision or nightmare. One was doubtful whether he had not in some way, unperceived, passed from time into eternity, in which the circumstances of his condition were a part of his new mode of being.

The following extract from the journal of the intrepid and enterprising Col. Fremont, will be interesting and appropriate in this connection:—

"We began," he says, "to be uneasy at Derosier's absence, fearing he might have been bewildered in the woods. Charles Towns, who had not yet recovered his mind, went to swim in the river, as if it were summer, and the stream placid, when it was a cold mountain torrent foaming among rocks. We were happy to see Derosier appear in the evening. He came in, and sitting down by the fire, began to tell us where he had been. He imagined he had been gone several days, and thought we were still at the camp where he had left us; and we were pained to see that his mind was deranged. It appeared that he had been lost in the mountain, and hunger and fatigue, joined to weakness of body, and fear of perishing in the mountains, had crazed him. The times were severe, when stout men lost their minds from extremity of suffering—when horses died—and when mules and horses, ready to die of starvation, were killed for food."

Some of the party, though sometimes, during brief intervals, perfectly sane, when awake, yet suffered from the most painful and terrifying dreams, in which they saw combats and heard cries of despair and anguish. Dreams of famine and death, of floundering in fathomless snows, frequently made them afraid to sleep; for when they did, they often started up from their miserable beds in horror and affright. These not only tormented the mind, but the body also was exhausted and fatigued, through the sympathy which exists between the mortal and immortal part of man's nature.

Some of these unhappy emigrants felt a general sinking of all the energies of the mind, and a total prostration of the body, without, however, experiencing any gnawing of hunger. The unfortunate Denton was probably an example of this. It will be recollected that he was found at one time asleep upon the snow. He was with great difficulty aroused, but was afterward left with a little food; and when found dead, the food left with him was in his pocket. It is probable that, after writing the piece of poetry which I have mentioned in a former part of this volume as having been discovered at his side, he did not experience a sensation of hunger; and a drowsiness overcoming him, he never awoke.

This absence of the sensation of hunger was generally followed by an irresistible desire to sleep. If great efforts were not made to arouse them from the torpor into which they were sinking, an unnatural and difficult manner of breathing was usually observed in about half an hour; and this was followed by a rattling of the throat in about three-fourths of an hour. This continued from one to four hours; when death closed the scene; the individual appearing to be in a profound slumber, until life was wholly extinct, and the spirit was released from its suffering body. Sometimes they were permitted thus to die, in order that the miserable survivors might in this manner obtain food, without resorting to a more horrid alternative. There were examples of no efforts being able to awaken persons from this dreadful slumber. On one occasion, a person in this sleep threw his arm out in such a manner that his hand fell into the fire. Mr. Eddy, who was awake, and observed it, hoped that it would awaken the miserable sleeper, and he permitted it to remain there until it was doubled and shriveled. He then threw the hand back upon the body; but the sleeper soon extended it again, and it fell into the fire, where it was consumed to a coal, without the slightest movement of a single muscle, or a perceptible change of the features, indicative of pain.

If the effort to arouse the sleeper was successful, as it frequently was, the poor sufferer often spoke of the most delightful visions, in which his imagination had presented to his view, beautiful plantations of luxuriantly growing crops, and tables groaning with a weight of food, prepared in the most inviting manner.

Such was the condition, both mental, and physical, into which Mr. Eddy felt himself sinking, at the time of his making his first meal of human flesh. He had ceased to experience the sensation of hunger, although at other times this had almost maddened him. But he felt a general prostration of body and mind, and a heaviness and lethargy almost imperceptibly stealing upon him. Those who were with him, told him that he was dying. This, however, he did not believe, but he, nevertheless, had witnessed enough to convince him that these were primary symptoms, which, if he did not resist them, would certainly terminate in his death in a few hours. He reasoned clearly concerning his condition, and he knew perfectly well that nothing but courage could rescue him from that state of stupor and mental imbecility into which he was falling.

A few became furious, and died without sinking into this slumber. Others died calm and peaceful, taking an affectionate leave of their friends, and expressing a confident hope in the mercy of the blessed Redeemer; and in the fullness of the provision made by His death for even the most wicked; and in His power and willingness to save them in His kingdom.

MRS. BRINN IN TRIBULATION.